WHITEMUD WALKING

MATTHEW JAMES WEIGEL

COACH HOUSE BOOKS, TORONTO

first edition

Canada Council for the Arts Conseil des Arts du Canada

ONTARIO ARTS COUNCIL
CONSEIL DES ARTS DE L'ONTARIO
an Ontario government agency
un organisme du gouvernement de l'Ontario

Canada

Published with the generous assistance of the Canada Council for the Arts and the Ontario Arts Council. Coach House Books also acknowledges the support of the Government of Canada through the Canada Book Fund and the Government of Ontario through the Ontario Book Publishing Tax Credit.

LIBRARY AND ARCHIVES CANADA CATALOGUING IN PUBLICATION

Title: Whitemud walking / Matthew James Weigel.
Names: Weigel, Matthew James.
Identifiers: Canadiana (print) 20210317507 | Canadiana (ebook) 20210317515 | ISBN 9781552454411(softcover) | ISBN 9781770567139 (PDF) | ISBN 9781770567122 (EPUB)
Subjects: LCGFT: Poetry. | LCGFT: Visual poetry. | LCGFT: Creative nonfiction.
Classification: LCC PS8645.E359 W45 2022 | DDC C811/.6—dc23

Whitemud Walking is available as an ebook: ISBN 978 1 77056 712 2 (EPUB), 978 1 77056 713 9 (PDF)

Purchase of the print version of this book entitles you to a free digital copy. To claim your ebook of this title, please email sales@chbooks.com with proof of purchase. (Coach House Books reserves the right to terminate the free digital download offer at any time.)

for my family
and for home
this place
this creek
this river

'On the sloping sides of the great valley and on the flats below
the coyotes barked and howled at night, but on the top of the bank
we taught ... we were the University of Alberta;

and we felt sure that the future belonged to us,
not to the coyotes.'

– R. K. Gordon, 'University Beginnings in Alberta'

'*shhh*
listen'

– Layli Long Soldier, *Whereas*

A NOTE AS WE BEGIN

I was born at the University of Alberta Hospital.
I earned my degrees here.

The university has much within its holdings and collections:

Land, parts of Whitemud Creek, parts of the mountains, parts of forests, treaty parchments, photos and audio recordings of my family, and also my very first chapbook of treaty poetry.

Some are on display and freely available to visit or view by the public.

Some are not.

This book began as thoughts on treaty and my obligations to the land in this time. But it spiralled outward into a journey of understanding of all my relations. This is a point of entry into these spaces I call home: myself, Whitemud Creek at Mactaggart Sanctuary, the Métis riverlots of the University of Alberta, and here at one of those places called a pêhonân on the river my family has travelled forever, kisiskâciwani-sîpiy. This journey extends in every direction outward and inward. To the mountains. To all the ocean. To the stories told and yet to be told in the sky and stars. To the little bits of everything inside me. To all of time and to my ancestors and my descendants. This is the network called upon in the treaties of this place.

In order to occupy territory, British law required Indigenous title to the land be extinguished through exchanges that went by the name of treaty. Following this practice, the United States made hundreds of such treaties with Indigenous nations. This lasted until an 1871 act of Congress made it illegal to recognize these nations as sovereign, ending the making of future treaties. That same summer, Canada and the Crown would begin the process of negotiating the numbered treaties of the North-West.

Here in the North-West, these rigorous negotiations by my ancestors and relations occurred in defence of a different expectation of the treaty-making process. Here, treaty means reciprocity and obligation. Here, treaty lasts forever.

But a separate system of title extinguishment was put in place for my Métis relations. The scrip system would deal with the Halfbreeds on a family-by-family basis, rather than nation-to-nation. Scrip were one-time grants of land or cash given to each head of family. Systemic fraud and white supremacy in the land grants office, enforced through military occupation, reduced a negotiated 1.4 million acres of Métis land in Manitoba to 200,000 acres. This violent dispossession would be repeated across the North-West from 1870 onward.

Just recently I marked the 100th anniversary of my great-great-grandfather signing the last of the numbered treaties of the North-West as a witness.

The ink is dry. The sheets are stained. The decorative gold of the paper marbling is oxidized a sickly green. The spine of the binding disintegrated.

Canada has neutralized its treaty obligations by treating them as historical and complete. So I call this a resistance historiography, a journey toward an Indigenous imaginary that de-historicizes and de-neutralizes the state's obligations to us. It is an imaginary that envisions and enacts the infinite incompleteness of treaty. Only in that expanse can a reciprocity and obligation as great as the North-West find its place.

My kin Hunter Cardinal described to me the Nêhiyaw concept of infinity: misewa, as 'all the stories that have been, continue to be, and those stories yet to be created.' It can be envisioned as a network of stories that spiral outward from me to my kin, my communities, my nations, the land, the cosmos.

The nature of this spiralling is also a returning. As the stories expand they revisit. In these back and forward movements each story leaves impressions on the others. And the world leaves marks upon them all. Sometimes these marks are left by the colonial extractive violence of government systems, of educational and archival institutions, of resource and energy corporations.

But, mostly, marks are left by this place around me, this waiting place, this pêhonân. These marks are a learning, a joy, an exercise of love and movement and patience and potential. These things and more I owe to this place. And it is so very beautiful here among the magpies.

PART ONE

WHETHER THEY TOOK TREATY OR NOT, THEY WERE SUBJECT TO THE LAWS OF THE DOMINION

Articles of a Treaty

t?app=fonandcol&id=3972485&lang=eng IT 255 3 August 1871 4 sheets; 49 x 61 cm (19
T 255 124 Surrender of land in consideration of reserves to be laid out in proportion to
er family of 5 plus additional land surrounding the reserve, $3.00 per person, schools etc
x seals on left edge of page one T-9939 2014.09.20 - 2015.09.20 Indian Treaty no. 1 1996.1
10.30 Western Treaty No. 1 - IT 255 RG 10, vol.1846 IT 256 IT 257 IT 258 - Map (c.181
ap (c.1871) IT 260 - Amendments 1875 IT 261 - Amendments 1875 IT 262 - Amendments
T-9939 T-9939 T-9939 T-9939 RG10 [Access 90 Open] [RG10] 1846/IT255 [Access 90 O
T-9939 [Access 90 Open] 2021-03-16 Western Treaty No. 6 IT 296 e002995351 e00299
5354 e002995355 e002995356 e002995357 e002995358 e002995359 e00299
5361 e002995362 e002995363 1876 RG10 1847/IT296 T-9940 3980032 http://central
a/.redirect?app=fonandcol&id=3980032&lang=eng 1876 10 sheets 44 x 56 cm (17-1/2" x
157A Surrender of land in consideration of reserves to be set aside in proportion to 1 sq
a family of 5, a one time payment of $12 per person, maintenance of schools, annual paym
g and fishing rights, etc. 121,000 square miles covering the central areas of Saskatche
erta one red wax seal one wide blue ribbon Two straight parallel holes are in each sheet
eft corner of page 19 is missing Page 19 also has the title of document on it T-9940 1876/0
76/08/28 and 1876/09/09 2015.09.20 - 2016.08.20 (first page with wax seal & ribbon
red Memories 5 2001.01.22 - 2001.11.12 (RG10 - Western Treaty No. 6 - IT 297) 2018.10
3.12 IT 297 IT 298 IT 299 - Adhesion 9 and 21 August 1877 IT 300 - Adhesion 25 Septer
T 301 - Adhesion 19 August 1878 IT 302 - Adhesion 29 August 1878 IT 303 - Adhesi
ber 1878 IT 304 - Adhesion 18 September 1878 IT 305 - Adhesion 2 July 1879 IT 3
on of 1882 IT 494 - IT 501 - Adhesions of 1944, 1950, 1954, 1956 T-9940 T-9940 T-9940 T-
RG10 [Access 90 Open] [RG10] 1847/IT296 [Access 90 Open] [RG10] T-9940 [Access 90 O
3-16 Printed copy of Western Treaty No. 6 - IT 297 e002995365 e002995366 1876 RG10 1
T-9940 3980041 http://central.bac-lac.gc.ca/.redirect?app=fonandcol&id=3980041&lang
T 297 1876 1 sheet; 74 x 49 cm (29" x 19-1/2") IT 297 157A Surrender of land in considera
rves to be set aside in proportion to 1 square mile to a family of 5, a one time payme
person, maintenance of schools, annual payments, hunting and fishing rights, etc. T-
8/23 and 1876/08/28 and 1876/09/09 IT 296 IT 298 IT 299 - Adhesion 9 and 21 Au
T 300 - Adhesion 25 September 1877 IT 301 - Adhesion 19 August 1878 IT 302 - Adhe
ust 1878 IT 303 - Adhesion 3 September 1878 IT 304 - Adhesion 18 September 1878 IT
ion 2 July 1879 IT 328 - Adhesion of 1882 IT 494 - IT 501 - Adhesions of 1944, 1950, 1
-9940 T-9940 T-9940 T-9940 T-9940 RG10 [Access 90 Open] [RG10] 1847/IT297 [Ac
n] [RG10] T-9940 [Access 90 Open] 2021-03-16 Western Treaty No. 8 - IT 415 e00299
6117 e002996118 e002996119 e002996120 e002996121 e002996122 e00299
6124 e002996125 1899 RG10 1851/IT415 T-9941 3986104 http://central.bac-lac.gc
t?app=fonandcol&id=3986104&lang=eng Western Treaty No. 8 - IT 415 1899 10 sheets; a
n (8" x 13") IT 415 428 T-9941 1899/06/21 1899/07/01 1899/07/08 2002.06.23 - 2002.1
No. 8) 1.4.1 Perspectives (Encroachment and Treaties) Pier 21 2015.05.05-2016.05.05 IT
ion 25 & 27 July 1899 IT 417 - adhesion 6 July 1899 IT 418 - adhesion 13 July 1899 IT
ion 17 July 1899 IT 420 - adhesion 4 August 1899 IT 421 - adhesion 14 August 1899 IT
n 8 June 1900 IT 423 - adhesion 30 May 1900 IT 424 - adhesion 23 June 1900 IT 425 - adhe
1900 IT 426 T-9941 T-9941 T-9941 T-9941 T-9941 RG10 [Access 90 Open] [RG10] 1
Access 90 Open] [RG10] T-9941 [Access 90 Open] 2021-03-16 e002996596 1921 RG10 1
T-9941 3988351 http://central.bac-lac.gc.ca/.redirect?app=fonandcol&id=3988351&lang
1921 29 x 38 cm (11-1/2" x 15") 21 sheets; 28 x 37 cm (11" x 14-1/2") IT 504 2398, 2
401, 2402, 2403, 2404, 2405 Conroy for King George V "Treaty Number Eleven" 372
miles lying roughly north of the 60th parallel and Treaty no. 8, south of the Arctic Oc
the northern portion of the Coppermine River and west of the northern Yukon bo
nd white seal with "RG 10 series 4, vol. 18" "Record Group 10 Series 4, Vol(s) 18"T-

INSIDE THE POP-UP BOX

I'm in the library canada keeps my kin in
and I've brought all the other libraries I've ever been in with me.

My mum's library,
where as a child I saw a pop-up dinosaur
and rows of shelving
and drawers I thought must hold so many fossils.

My dad's library of tapes in the car,
and my favourite songs are the ones that tell a story,
and we drive all day,
and my dad tells stories.

And I thought,
every story must be a layer in the earth of stories,

and I thought,
it's the stories in front of you that you remember the best.

And so this time I'm in a library, it's full of glass to let the sun in,
but all the books are in metal boxes in stacks
in rows of other metal boxes,
all inside this concrete box.

And the glass walls let the sun in, and it's warm in there,
and I am warm, holding my coat and my sweater and my bag
and all the other things that aren't my name.
That, I write on the clipboard,
and it is not lost on me that I am here to see
my great-great-grandfather's signature,
and that I must offer mine to the library first.

In this library they hold the layers of the thing called canada.
They keep it in a vault and behind it is another vault,
across it is another row of vaults
and I can see the vaults but no, I cannot see the vaults.

Beyond us is the new building,
the building they say will be staffed with robots,
arms of a safe temperature
reminding us
that to touch a document is to take a piece of it with you
and to leave a piece of you behind,
and it is this exchange we must climate control,
in de-reciprocal programming.
And when only the dead and programmed can see my kin,
no one will see my kin.

See me, my layers,
A PROCLAMATION. By the KING,
with a line down its centre.
And this layer is the treaty,
this layer is the treaty,
this layer is the treaty that cuts through the centre of me.
Whereas in a line of red ink beneath,
whereas in a red ink, Her Majesty,
whereas I am a measure of a constitution,
my kin and marked by hand,
tooled in a border of fading gold foil,
and with a spine no longer structural,
but splayed (*pro pelle cutem*) on a table.
And numbered.

archive this book

erase it

FORT EDMONTON WAS ESTABLISHED FOR
THE HVDSON'S BAY COMPANY IN 1795
BY WILLIAM TOMISON THE COMPANY
AS FVR TRADER AND MERCHANT HAS SINCE
BEEN ACTIVE IN LIFE OF THIS COMMVNITY

TO BE A THING UNFINISHED

FOR
THE   COMPANY
BY   THE   COMPANY

ANCESTORS OF AUTHOR DETERMINED (TO BE A GOOD ANCESTOR)

I'd like you to see some of my family. This is Marie Fabien and James Balsillie with four of their youngest children.

When I showed the image to my dad, he got quiet, tears in his eyes and with his hand held to his face.

This photograph is not in the possession of my family, but in the archives of the University of Alberta.

I've never seen the photo. Neither has my father or anyone else in my family. I found it online. The image has an item number and subject taxonomy links to 'Family and personal life' and 'Aboriginal Peoples.'

I assume it sits in a box on a shelf.

FAMILY PHOTOS

There's a baby picture of me on a polar-bear-skin rug.
Dad loves to tell that story.
I didn't have a diaper on,
and he just laughs and laughs,
you can imagine how much my auntie was freaking out.

Who am I to the fur trade?
Who is this naked baby on a bear-skin rug,
surrounded by laughter and aunties?

Who am I to a country in its infant nationalism?

LIST OF RULES I HAVE BROKEN IN THE ARCHIVE

I have gotten, on occasion, too close to the materials I study.
I am the materials I study.

I have taken photos with an unsupported camera,
the motion photos saved a record of the shaking of my hands.

I have cried in the archive.

ACTS RESPECTING VIOLENCE TO THE NORTH-WEST

1870	Rupert's Land Transfer
1871	Treaty No. 1
1871	Treaty No. 2
1873	Treaty No. 3
1874	Treaty No. 4
1875	Treaty No. 5
1876	Treaty No. 6
1877	Treaty No. 7
1899	Treaty No. 8
1905	Treaty No. 9
1906	Treaty No. 10
1921	Treaty No. 11

Fort Garry attacked by the Canadian government.

Prime Minister Macdonald caught taking bribes from railway financiers to get re-elected.

In which The Company sells land it does not own.

' ... surrender and yield up to the Government of the Dominion of Canada, for Her Majesty the Queen and Her successors forever ... '

– Treaty No. 6

' ... whether they took treaty or not, they were subject to the laws of the Dominion.'

– *Report of the Commissioner for Treaty No. 11*

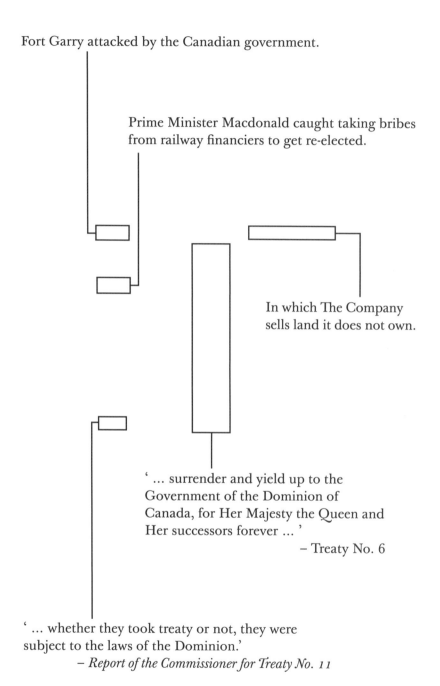

WHITEMUD WALKING

'This Sanctuary was donated to the University of Alberta by Sandy A. Mactaggart and the Province of Alberta ... the Sanctuary has been made available for the enjoyment of the public, on the basis that it remains a Sanctuary where unspoiled nature takes precedence over people. Please help us to protect and preserve this area by leaving it as you have found it.'

– Mactaggart Sanctuary, University of Alberta

I

My home is triangulated by the convergence of Whitemud Creek and Blackmud Creek. To get to Mactaggart Sanctuary I cross 119th Street westward. As I cross the street I leave the Papaschase Cree Reserve, where I live on land the city annexed through fraud. Mactaggart Sanctuary is in Treaty 6 territory, and Métis Nation of Alberta region 4, but is in the holdings of the University of Alberta.

RELEVANT FACTS AND NUMERALS OF TREATY AND MÉTIS SCRIP

Your inquiry to Library and Archives Canada reference number: QMS-105752.

Your user card number to access Library and Archives Canada: 23286003012896.

Items I would like to see:

Treaty 11 book (IT 504).
Treaty 11 adhesion sheet (IT 505).
Treaty 6 manuscript (IT 296).
Treaty 6 print copy (IT 297).
Treaty 6 print copy (IT 298).
Scrip affidavit for Adelaide Balsillie (1499402).
Scrip claim and investigation for J. A. R. Balsillie (1497707).

SELF-SERVE PHOTOGRAPHY APPLICATION

User first, name last,
shaded area to be filled out by staff,
this photocopy is so faded, there is nothing shaded
it has the broken texted signature of a copy of a copy,
this green page is my copy:

1. RG15 1319 Restrictions 90 verified
2. RG15 1372 Restrictions 90 verified
3.
4.
5.
6.
7.
8.

Terms of governance, of reproduction, of use, of material, of collections, of Library and Archives Canada:

On the basis of my representations I will not use these collections in a manner that would infringe the rights of others, of liability assumed in full, the library accepts no responsibility, bears no responsibility, shall not be liable, shall face no consequence of flow of information under its control.

An act a term a governing reproduction, a use a basis a subject a statistical purpose, a good faith request in accordance with these acts, a validation, a claim, a dispute, a grievance of any of the aboriginal peoples of Canada.

A version of this form, a flag in the shape of a dot being squeezed above the final letter. Canada warrants, collects, uses, archives, infringes, assumes, authorizes, accepts, accesses, acts, maintains, protects, represents, discloses.

I print I number I date I sign.

NORTH-WEST HISTORIOGRAPHY

'Long ago, there was no difference whether you were Dene or Métis. When we would come in from the bush, George Norn used to play the fiddle ... we danced all night.'

– Ft. Resolution Elder,
Royal Commission on Aboriginal Peoples

'In 1900, Fort Resolution Indians wanted [Pierre Beaulieu] to be their Chief, but the Treaty Commission did not accept his election because he was a Métis.'

– René Fumoleau,
As Long As This Land Shall Last

'The Métis and treaty families are all related. We are just like one family and we used to help each other in the old days. It's still like that. The Treaty didn't make a difference in how we got along. After the Treaty, the people did whatever they had done before.'

– Albert Fabien,
That's the Way We Lived: An Oral History of the Fort Resolution Elders

'No difference. Just one big family that shared everything.'

– Jim Weigel,
my dad

PLACE OF CREATION: NO PLACE, UNKNOWN, OR UNDETERMINED

Individual case files – Enfranchisements – Elsie (Norn) Weigel Snowdrift Band – District of Mackenzie

[Access 32 Restricted by law]

Record Information – Details:
This is my grandmother's enfranchisement file. I've never seen it. I've only just seen this archive catalogue entry for the first time. I know about Łútsël K'é, which was Snowdrift. Grandma was adopted. I know about her name, which was Norn. My cousin told me my uncle said Grandma never had status. I just assumed she did, but lost it when she married Grandpa. I never met Grandpa. Sometimes family just doesn't know. I wonder about who the archive is for. I can see that a file exists but I can't see it. It tells me that the file's place of creation is of 'no place, unknown, or undetermined.' Tell me about it. Sometimes family just doesn't know. I can see all these numbers inscribed on the catalogue entry. Container notes: M-2523 M-2523 M-2523. Finding aid: 10-727. I can click on the 10-727. It takes me to a collection search that shows me 842 files. A lot of them seem to also be enfranchisement files. Usually the word 'enfranchisement' means something like liberation, or the gaining of privilege or voting rights. But for First Nations folks it specifically means to lose Indian status. To be compulsorily de-registered. There have been several ways to become enfranchised over the history of the Indian Act: obtaining a university degree, becoming a doctor or lawyer, taking religious orders, leaving the country for long periods without getting permission from the department. If you were enfranchised, your children were also automatically enfranchised. And like my grandmother, if you married a white man you and your descendents were enfranchised and the government waived its treaty obligations to you and your family. In this way, the state continues its goals of extinguishing rights. My grandmother was the only grandparent I ever really knew. I remember being in Hay River with her, at a table with her sisters. The kitchen was full of laughter. There was a special kind of joy in her face when she was home that I never knew here. I miss her every day.

No. 3 claim of

a Half-Breed head.

ADELAIDE ROWAND

I, of the parish
of the county
of said Province
in Dominion in

I am the Half-breed myself
I claim I was born and I have not
nor have I claimed
or received as an Indian

I was born on or about.

And on the 15th day of July, A.D. 1870,
when Canada made of itself entitled to the North-West
and Queen Victoria herself and her successors forever and ever,
I was resident in Manitoba,
and I claim to be entitled as such.

Myself and husband and child
my parents were
my father a halfbreed
and my mother a halfbreed

having been first read and explained
seeming perfectly to understand the same
and signed,

Adelaide Rowand:
No claim of a half-breed head.

HUNT UP THE HALF-BREED WHOSE SCRIP THIS WAS

It isn't just the government that wants your land,
and it isn't just the railway,
but an irrational invasion of elm trees
on the road where I wonder which street sign is real.

I paraphrase a lawyer hunting,
but he died in 1928 and I am of a stolen sentiment,
engraved in the buffalo hunt
worth something like 160 dollars or 160 acres.
Less in 1870s prices.
Less in 1900s prices.
Less in today's prices or in today's sentiments.

And I paraphrase him hunting, who died in 1928,
and who did not take the idea of a railway scandal with him
who said, hunt up the halfbreed whose scrip this was.

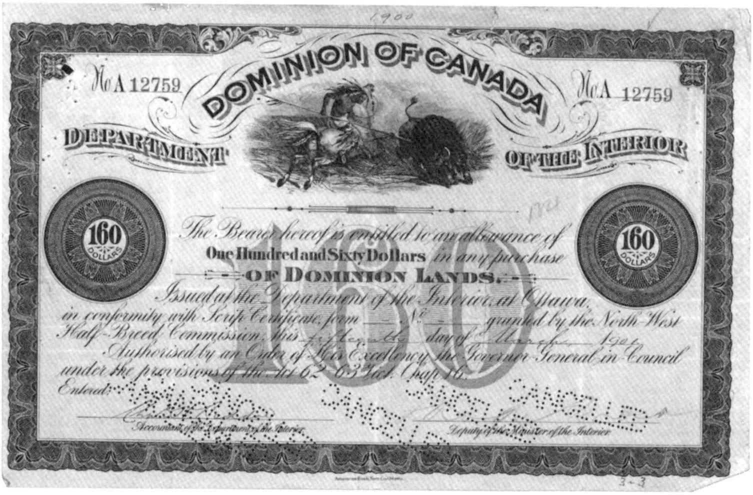
No. A 12759 DOMINION OF CANADA No. A 12759

DEPARTMENT OF THE INTERIOR

160 DOLLARS

The Bearer hereof is entitled to an allowance of
One Hundred and Sixty Dollars in any purchase
OF DOMINION LANDS.

Issued at the Department of the Interior, at Ottawa,
in conformity with Scrip Certificate, form ___ No. ___ granted by the North-West
Half-Breed Commission this [illegible] day of [illegible] [illegible]
Authorised by an Order of His Excellency the Governor-General in Council
under the provisions of the Act 62-63 Vict. Chap. 16.

Entered: CANCELLED

Accountant of the Department of the Interior

Deputy of the Minister of the Interior

American Bank Note Co. Ottawa.

3-3

CONCERNING HIS CLAIM TO PARTICIPATE (1497707)

21. State anything bearing on your claim that you may wish? *I do not know that I have ever received script. And I wish to be treated the same as other people have been treated.*

CONCERNING HER CLAIM TO PARTICIPATE (1497707)

21. State anything bearing on your claim that you may wish? *In 1900 I appeared before Mr. McRae (?) and signed an application for my halfbreed script. No action was apparently taken on my application as Mr. Conroy in 1901 did not give my script as previous to this on July 2, 1901 I was married to James Allen Balsillie and was at Simpson enroute to Fort Nelson when script was paid. I later met Mr. Conroy at Liard on his way to Fort Nelson where he was paying treaty and told me that he had carried my script for about three years and he failed to locate me. He did not have my script with him then but promised to look it up and bring it in on his next trip. I again met him in 1913 at Providence, I did not speak to him about my script but my husband who went with him as far as Fort Smith did so and he was informed that he would look into the matter. I spoke to him again at Providence in 1921 and he informed me that a man by the name of Taylor in Edmonton had papers signed by myself and husband handing over my script dated at Nelson. I never signed these papers because I never had received script and moreover no white man ever put his feet in Fort Nelson during my stay there. In 1921 I took an affidavit to this effect before Mr. Jack Cory who was on the LeBeaux case in Providence and at the same time put in my second application for script. I am quite willing that you search your records and try and find the papers I am supposed to have signed. If they are found I am willing to take any affidavit that you wish that said signature is a forgery and I consider that I should not be held accountable for any such forgeries.*

1921
Halfbreed commissioner is convinced the wife and children are entitled to the grant of 240$ each.

1924
Controller notes, if the mother's claim is again to be re-considered and this time allowed, the claims of the ten children born after the original claim will require re-consideration.

14. What are their names, dates of birth and names of birthplace?

John, George	Balsillie	1902	at Fort Nelson		
Edward	"	1903	"	"	"
Beatrice	"	1905	"	"	Liard
James	"	1907	"	"	"
Harry	"	1909	"	"	"
Fredrick	"	1911	"	"	"
Clarence	"	1913	"	"	"
Ernest	"	1915	"	Providence	
Harold	"	1917	"		"
Hugh	"	1919	"		"

1927
Deputy minister of the interior calls my attention to the fact that there is no more land to give the halfbreeds. The act was repealed a few years ago.

2020
The archives asks for justification to see records.

2021
Department tells me to have Dad call the entitlement unit.

FILL OUT THIS FORM

please select one:
O First Nations
O Métis
O Inuit

II

I now cherish each attempt by a mosquito to bite me, understanding as I do that there are fewer insects every year than the last. I wonder about nineteenth-century anxieties of buffalo, and I cherish the remaining buffalo. And caribou. And all the sovereign plant and animal nations not mentioned in the treaty 6 document, but who are part of the treaty nonetheless.

RELEVANT FACTS AND NUMERALS OF TREATY AND MÉTIS SCRIP

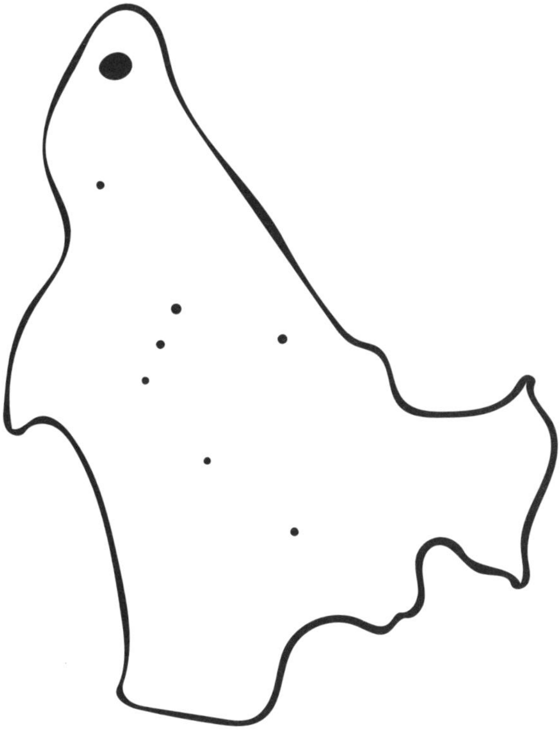

MAP ILLUSTRATING THE DISAPPEARANCE OF THE BISON

1870: QUEEN VICTORIA ACQUIRES AD NAUSEUM

This photograph of the throne at Windsor Castle was taken by André Adolfe Eugène Disdéri. As with other things, the photo was acquired by Queen Victoria in 1870. The Travancore Throne is a masterwork of carved ivory, gold, precious stones, and silk, crafted in southern India and gifted to Her Majesty for presentation at the Great Exhibition of 1851. She called it her 'magnificent chair.' When she became the Empress of India, she had her photo taken seated on this throne.

Also in 1870, in this throne room, Her Majesty, along with the Lord President, the Lord Privy Seal, the Lord Chamberlain, and a Mr. Gladstone, made official the Rupert's Land and North-Western Territory Order. This order placed some four million square kilometres of this continent under the legislative control of the Dominion of Canada. For the two centuries previous, that area had been under the commercial purview of the Governor and Company of Adventurers of England, Trading into Hudson's Bay.

I have acquired and used this photograph without permission. It has been digitally altered to suit my needs.

III

I was digging through company documentation and order in council records. I had to stop. I was sobbing. All I could think about was Queen Victoria sitting in a room in Windsor Castle with a handful of lords around her as they turned a land she had never seen into lines and numbers.

RELEVANT FACTS AND NUMERALS OF TREATY AND MÉTIS SCRIP

Total surface area of water in Denendeh: 163,021 km^2.

Total surface area of land in England: 130,279 km^2.

WE DROWNED THE LAND OF ENGLAND IN THE WATERS OF DENENDEH

It was clearly understood,
there was no ownership of land,
so clearly does the land, in fact, own me.

My water from the river and my nitrogen,
a buffalo protein.
I am a fleshbound manuscript of what this place might say.
Hear in it how family made the treaties, live them, love the land,
this place this creek this river.

Make a sediment of me, make mud, make silt and send it on its way:
Saskatchewan
Athabasca
Slave
Mackenzie to the sea.

If you could take the dirt of England and rejuvenate the ground,
if you could manage, as was always done,
as people and the beavers manage,
take the soil of England,
cast it in the lakes across the north,
and ball it up in handfuls,
homes, and dams,
and hold the land of England to account
for Canada,
for the bishopry,
for the Company,
and record it in the manuscript of the north-west.

Then write these things that we are saying down,
write them on two sheets,
one for you and one for me to keep.

Hold these things we learn and teach them on,
tell the story written in the mud,
recorded in the river,
and copied days downstream.

Then I would hope you carry safe your copy,
and when you reach the sea,
find England,
compare it with this copy we have made,
and stir the ocean with it.

PÊHONÂN

'I will ask the interpreter to read to you what has been written,
and before I go away I will have a copy made
to leave with the principal Chiefs.'

– Alexander Morris,
Commissioner, Treaty No. 6

Did you know where the river would take you when you first saw it?
Watched it bend toward you, wrap you up in school and bridges
in a loop.
Watched it swim away, even as it still holds you.

Wait here, this is where we'll meet
at pêhonân.

Did you know how much you would resemble an ocean?
Gather everything, who you are,
wait and gather wait and gather.

These are things the river says here,
speaks again downstream,
wait and gather wait and gather
stories, gather
witness, gather
sharing.

touch the pencil
make your mark
negotiate
agree

Did you know that when you wrote this down the river would
remember it?

THIS STORY IS CALLED: THE PRISON WARDEN BOUGHT MY UNCLE'S BUFFALO AND SOLD THEM TO LORD STRATHCONA

– until there were almost no buffalo left.

They say the last buffalo to be born on the plain was in the care of a great-uncle of mine, James McKay, at Deer Lodge, on the Assiniboine River.

Policy and industry murdered the great herds, and the land was changing, trees were being planted. My great-uncle would take home calves orphaned in the hunt.

When he died, the small herd was auctioned off to the prison warden, a Canadian soldier who came to the North-West to kill Métis and, after, settled in the north-west.

But the buffalo would not be kept in the prison long, the warden owed Lord Strathcona money and sold the buffalo to him.

Like all tycoons, Strathcona had no use for buffalo and so he gave them to the national park in the Rocky Mountains. The last buffalo to be born on the plain they named Sir Donald after Lord Strathcona.

Tourists came to take his photo. And when he died, the government took his head and stuffed it, hung it on the wall of the Banff superintendent's office.

I am told it may have been discarded after being eaten by the mice who took residence in the head.

1876: TREATY NO. 6

I wake up at 6am to a weight on my chest.
I massage it until it says the word ‘treaty.’

1876 and my uncle is at pêhonân,
signs the treaty with a leftward slant.
It is August and the aspens bend in the wind.

Dreamt I was in a library again,
walking down the stairs into the basement,
walking down the stairs into the earth.
I see the treaty parchment on a wooden table,
it comes as no surprise the land herself holds this knowledge.

TREATY NO. 6

ARTICLES OF A TREATY made and concluded near Carlton on the 23rd day of August and on the 28th day of said month, respectively, and near Fort Pitt on the 9th day of September, in the year of Our Lord one thousand eight hundred and seventy-six, between Her Most Gracious Majesty the Queen of Great Britain and Ireland, by Her Commissioners, the Honourable Alexander Morris, Lieutenant-Governor of the Province of Manitoba and the North-west Territories, and the Honourable James McKay, and the Honourable William Joseph Christie, of the one part, and the Plain and Wood Cree and the other Tribes of Indians, inhabitants of the country within the limits hereinafter defined and described by their Chiefs, chosen and named as hereinafter mentioned, of the other part.

Whereas the Indians inhabiting the said country have, pursuant to an appointment made by the said Commissioners, been convened at meetings at Fort Carlton, Fort Pitt and Battle River, to deliberate upon certain matters of interest to Her Most Gracious Majesty, of the one part, and the said Indians of the other.

And whereas the said Indians have been notified and informed by Her Majesty's said Commissioners that it is the desire of Her Majesty to open up for settlement, immigration and such other purposes as to Her Majesty may seem meet, a tract of country bounded and described as hereinafter mentioned, and to obtain the consent thereto of Her Indian subjects inhabiting the said tract, and to make a treaty and arrange with them, so that there may be peace and good will between them and Her Majesty, and that they may know and be assured of what allowance they are to count upon and receive from Her Majesty's bounty and benevolence.

And whereas the Indians of the said tract, duly convened in council, as aforesaid, and being requested by Her Majesty's said Commissioners to name certain Chiefs and Headmen, who should be authorized on their behalf to conduct such negotiations and sign any treaty to be founded thereon, and to become responsible to Her Majesty for their faithful performance by their respective Bands of such obligations as shall be assumed by them, the said Indians have thereupon named for that purpose, that is to say, representing the Indians who make the treaty at Carlton, the several Chiefs and Councillors who have subscribed hereto, and representing the Indians who make the treaty at Fort Pitt, the several Chiefs and Councillors who have subscribed hereto.

And thereupon, in open council, the different Bands having presented their Chiefs to the said Commissioners as the Chiefs and Headmen, for the purposes aforesaid, of the respective Bands of Indians inhabiting the said district hereinafter described.

And whereas, the said Commissioners then and there received and acknowledged the persons so presented as Chiefs and Headmen, for the purposes aforesaid, of the respective Bands of Indians inhabiting the said district hereinafter described.

And whereas, the said Commissioners have proceeded to negotiate a treaty with the said Indians, and the same has been finally agreed upon and concluded, as follows, that is to say:

The Plain and Wood Cree Tribes of Indians, and all other the Indians inhabiting the district hereinafter described and defined, do hereby cede, release, surrender and yield up to the Government of the Dominion of Canada, for Her Majesty the Queen and Her successors forever, all their rights, titles and privileges, whatsoever, to the lands included within the following limits, that is to say:

Commencing at the mouth of the river emptying into the north-west angle of Cumberland Lake; thence westerly up the said river to its source; thence on a straight line in a westerly direction to the head of Green Lake; thence northerly to the elbow in the Beaver River; thence down the said river northerly to a point twenty miles from the said elbow; thence in a westerly direction, keeping on a line generally parallel with the said Beaver River (above the elbow), and about twenty miles distant therefrom, to the source of the said river; thence northerly to the north-easterly point of the south shore of Red Deer Lake, continuing westerly along the said shore to the western limit thereof; and thence due west to the Athabasca River; thence up the said river, against the stream, to the Jaspar House, in the Rocky Mountains; thence on a course south-easterly, following the easterly range of the mountains, to the source of the main branch of the Red Deer River; thence down the said river, with the stream, to the junction therewith of the outlet of the river, being the outlet of the Buffalo Lake; thence due east twenty miles; thence on a straight line south-eastwardly to the mouth of the said Red Deer River on the south branch of the Saskatchewan River; thence eastwardly and northwardly, following on the boundaries of the tracts conceded by the several treaties numbered four and five to the place of beginning.

And also, all their rights, titles and privileges whatsoever to all other lands wherever situated in the North-west Territories, or in any other Province or portion of Her Majesty's Dominions, situated and being within the Dominion of Canada.

The tract comprised within the lines above described embracing an area of 121,000 square miles, be the same more or less.

To have and to hold the same to Her Majesty the Queen and Her successors forever.

And Her Majesty the Queen hereby agrees and undertakes to *lay aside*

r e se r v e s fo r

lands ..

ON THE BOUNDARIES OF TREATY NO. 6

commencing to the place of beginning;
emptying;

in 1959 the South Saskatchewan river was dammed;
forever altering the boundary of Treaty no. 6;
such that it technically no longer exists;

westerly to the western limit, thence due west;
emptying;
to the source;

it must also be noted that the treaty negotiations
did not include any discussion of water;
or mountains;
precisely those features chosen by the crown
to mark the boundaries of treaty;
making the boundaries a sort of negative space;

to the Athabasca, the Red Deer;
to the Buffalo;
Saskatchewan, the Beaver;
up, against the stream to the Green Lake;
and to the Rocky Mountains;

(the semi-colon marks when a complete sentence is being added to;
changed;)

emptying;

ecologists speak of metaphorical n-dimensional objects
that define our niche;
abstract objects defining our abstract place in ecological space;
defined by what is around us;

on a course north-west, northerly, north-easterly, easterly, south-easterly, south;
to the junction, the elbow, the head, the mouth;
to the source and the place of beginning.

emptying.

IV

Small yellow flowers line the path. One green spider and one caterpillar on one pink flower. Two cans of spray paint. Two brown spiders with black stripes at the water. One block of polystyrene foam floating. Patches of sweet clover. Repeated rapid ticking and the thump of a dragonfly striking a broad leaf. An orange-capped plastic drink bottle. Four angling spruce trees casting one shadow over the deep part of the rapids. One uncapped marker pen. Thirty more dragonflies crossing the water thirty feet above.

RELEVANT FACTS AND NUMERALS OF TREATY AND MÉTIS SCRIP

What remains of the book itself weighs: 703 g.

PART TWO

THE BUFFALO WILL SOON BE EXTERMINATED

Should you be one of the few given access to see the sixth of the numbered treaties you would be forgiven for thinking that the large pieces of paper with ink written on them are the actual treaty itself.

In truth the agreement exists as an embodiment of ceremony and lived movement within the framework of laws that extend throughout this territory called treaty six.

The spirit and intent of this has been acknowledged by both the Crown and the Crown in Canada.

The text is not the treaty.

When academics speak about books they sometimes use words like paratext to talk about the material that surrounds the text.

What follows is a paratext of treaty six.

I use Commissioner and Lieutenant-Governor Alexander Morris's 1880 book describing the crown's view of the treaty negotiations as a way for you to hold that paratext.

The margins of that book invite you to the gutter of this one.

Behind this through the middle and out the spine is the treaty.

CHA

THE TREATIES AT FC

-

The treaties made at Fort
1876, were of a very i
The great region covered
included in Treaties Numb
an area of approximately 1
vast extent of fertile territo
nation. The Crees had, very
North-West Territories to C
ance with the Government.
Simpson, the Indian Comm
tary of State in a despatch o
used the following language
"I desire also to call the at
state of affairs in the Indian
The intelligence that Her M
pewa Indians has already r
Blackfeet tribes. In the neig
the Saskatchewan, there is
of miners and other white
Mr. W. J. Christie, the office
District, that a treaty with t
least an assurance during t
shortly be made, is essential
tention, of the country. I wo

Butler, and to the enclosed
ie, the officer above alluded

etter from Mr. Christie, then
y Company, and subsequent-
ers, in which, he forwarded
fs to Lieut.-Gov. Archibald,
ive at Fort Garry, Red River
essages are as follows.

MONTON HOUSE, *13th April, 1871.*

om the Cree Chiefs, representing the
anied by a few followers.
whether their lands had been sold
Canadian Government in relation to
had raged throughout the past sum-
poverty of their country, the visible
port, ending by requesting certain
their case before Her Majesty's rep-
have reached these Indians through
of the North-West Territories to the
st anxious to hear from myself what

nt had as yet made no application for
en anything was required of them,
t beforehand to treat with them, and
et and live at peace with all men. I
s with Indians, heretofore, had dealt
were now in settled houses and well
with them the same liberal policy

any exaggerated stories about the
nity of telling them why troops had
to the Saskatchewan, it was as much
man, and that they would be for the

explanations offered, and said they
ands were complied with, and pres-
owers, and for the young men left in

camp, they departed well pleased fo
the future. At a subsequent intervi
that I should write down their wor
Red River. I accordingly did so, anc
ered. Copies of the proclamation is
liquors to Indians or others, and th
animal life, have been received, and
any power to enforce these laws, it is
I take this opportunity of most ear
ny's servants, and settlers in this c
and property here as soon as poss
speak with the Indians on behalf of

MEMORANDA:

Had I not complied with the de
little presents–and otherwise satisf
have proceeded to acts of violenc
would have been the beginning of
when it would have ended.

The buffalo will soon be extermi
Plain Indian tribes will fall back on
for relief and assistance. If not comp
provision for them, they will most a
no force or any law up there to pro
submit to be pillaged, or lose their
property, against such fearful odds

Gold may be discovered in paying
of the Rocky Mountains. We have, in
close to our boundary line, a large
only waiting and watching to hear
katchewan, and, without any form
there, or force to protect whites or
result.

I think that the establishment of
trict, as early as possible, is of most
try and the interest of Canada, and
ment with the Indians who inhabit

W. J. CHRIS
In

ns, Saskatchewan, to His Excellency
representative at Fort Garry, Red

e country.
ou, and bid you welcome. We heard
we don't want to sell our lands; it is
ell them.
ring animals, hitherto our sole sup-
p–we want you to pity us. We want
d assistance in everything when we
ble to support us.
arvation. We have had great starva-
ok away many of our people, the old,

coming to trade on our lands, and
o our enemies the Blackfeet.
ackfeet. Our young men are foolish,

o speak with us. If you can't come

. Christie, in whom we have every

e never shed any white man's blood,
whites, and want workmen, carpen-
settle. I want all my brother, Sweet

d River, treat me as a brother, that

k upon you, as if I saw you; I want
e the ground for myself and descen-

ready elsewhere stated, had
vith these Indians, and the
impressed upon the Privy
ernor of the North-West Ter-
n command of the Mounted

Police therein. The Ministe
Mills, in his Report for the
subject:

"Official reports received
ernor Morris and Colonel
mand of the Mounted Polic
showed that a feeling of
vailed very generally amon
lying in the unceded terri
and the Rocky Mountains.
prevailed amongst these In
been increased by the prese
tory of the parties engaged
graph line, and in the surve
also of a party belonging to
this state of feeling, and to
ty of the Indian tribes to th
Government, His Honor Go
tained authority to despatch
Indians the assurance that
this summer, to negotiate a
been done with their brethr

"The Rev. George McDou
a missionary amongst the
teen years, and who posse
was selected by His Honor t
Indians, a task which he pe
success: being able to repo
he found the feeling of dis
among the Indian tribes, h
remove it by his assuranc
during the coming year.

"For the purpose of negot

urself of the services of His
ad been formerly employed
Three, Four and Five. With
mes McKay and W. J. Chris-
considerable experience in
eover an intimate acquain-
Saskatchewan, their wants,

ge McDougall,* I may here
was made to him, to visit
Saskatchewan Valley, he was
his distant mission, among
ky Mountains, after a brief
io, but on the request being
ndians the intentions of the
ok the duty, and leaving his
the long journey, which his
him a letter missive from
he North-West Territories,
Commissioners would visit
er, to confer with them as to
and of the tidings which he
Indians were at once tran-
nfidence, the coming of the
ch he discharged his import-
h followed his exertions, will
to his Report, addressed to
results of his arduous mis-

mely death on the plains during the
ay to his camp, he was found lying
wilds was closed a most useful

he was found lying

MORLEYVILLE,

TO HIS HONOR LIEUTENANT-GO

Sir,–In accordance with my instr
possible to Carlton, in the neighbo
of Crees. From these I ascertained
much more arduous than I had exp
be found on the south branch of t
was also informed by these India
were united on two points: 1st. Tha
Government until a definite time f
plored the necessity of resorting t
mous in their determination to opp
roads through their country, until
them had been effected. I was furth
with the whites was likely to arise
who were anxious to make themse
large camps being much more mo
be the fact, I revolved to visit ever
in order that your Honor may for
towards the Government, I will giv
message was read. Mistahwahsis, h
ing the principal Chief of the Assi
is just it, that is all we wanted." T
heart is full of gratitude, foolish m
send his young men to our country
he would laugh at us, but this lett
justly toward us."

Beardy, or the Hairy Man, Chief
these words spoken by the Great Q
more implicit faith than I do now."
when I reached the Plain Crees, but
requested me to convey to the Gre
presents received, and they express
In a word, I found the Crees reason
in peace with the white men. I foun
the lead in their council. He forme
has been regarded as a troubleso
none of the Queen's presents; when
all round, but when the fox gets in
want no bait, let your Chiefs come

western country, and some of them

hed to take a claim at the crossing
f the Indians, one of my Saulteaux
to the east, said: "Do you see that
g?" "No," said the speculator. "I do,"
he multitude behind him, and when
nd take up all the land claims you
up no stakes in our country." It was
is party were a very small minority
driven them out of camp long ago,
y are noted conjurers.
council and which will be brought
their own language. "Tell the Great
rohibited bringing spirits into our
it, and it destroys us; when we do
for us a strong law, prohibiting the
ost exterminated the animals of our
with our white neighbors. We fur-
applicable to the Half-breed and In-
our forest or plain. Not many years
evolence of an enemy, now every one
r large numbers of valuable animals
ld farther ask that our chiefships be
ears almost every trader sets up his
n up into little parties, and our best
in connection with this, some of the
through this country, all calculated
rhood of Carlton an interested party
he Willow Indians that I had $3,000
vernment, and nothing in my long
the manner in which these Indians
of my letter of instructions. At the
alf-breeds greatly agitated. A gentle-
told them that the Mounted Police
killing buffalo or other animals, ex-
d these are only samples of the false
ejoice to witness a conflict of races.
ely, these are ample proofs.
s time that parties have been turned
ntaining supplies for the telegraph
met by three Indians and ordered to
the matter and listening to the state-

ments of all parties concerned, my
Indians would have regarded the
have not met with a Chief who wou
Personally I am indebted both t
Company's officials for their assist
Believing it would be satisfactory tc
sioners, I have kept the number of
places where I met the Indians.
By reckoning eight persons to e
imate to the number of Indians to
There may have been a few tents in
Crees at Lesser Slave Lake and La
twenty tents.
All of which is respectfully subm

The Commissioners, in
to travel through the prair
nation and returning to W
miles. They first met the In
ton, on the Saskatchewan
and eventually succeeded c
effecting a treaty with the I
28th of the same month w
negotiations were difficult
Mills, then Minister of th
thus characterizes them:–"
dians of the Saskatchewan
extravagant demands whic
certain points, it needed a
discretion, of which the Co
bring the negotiations to a

The number of Indians, as estima
him, was 3,976.

ed chiefly at Carlton: The
estly disposed to treat, and
ıd Ah-tuk-uh-koop, shewed
t desire to come to an un-

ver, by the action of the Wil-
ance of one of their Chiefs,
to the progress of the trea-
uncil, unless it was held at
where the Chief pretended
vision that the treaty was
re, moreover, under the in-
Saulteaux, the chief portion
s of the other treaties, and
lesome. Before the arrival
eaux conceived the idea of
nch Half-breeds, the Crees,
crossing of the Saskatche-
or, and his entrance into
le the proposal first to the
d to undertake it, and then
in silence. One of them at
River Saskatchewan, said,
er?" The answer was, "No,"
can you stop the progress
Commissioners arrived at
from the Crees met them,
was not needed. About a
mbled at the crossing, and
r, had the right of passage,
or of Messrs. Christie and
other Commissioner, Mr.
next day, having proceeded

by another route, and there
who at once asked the Li
treaty at the hill, near the
replied, that he would mee
desired, but must first go
he had appointed. An escor
Commissioners at Duck La
ton, in consequence of the
of the threatened interfer
several days' delay the Com
the Crees without the Wil
ence had opened, the Bea
informed of the terms the
in advance. The reply was t
the other Indians, and rep
as it was his own fault tha
part in the proceedings. Th
etly and deliberately, the C
all the time they desired. T
their future. They saw the
away, and they were anxio
large terms granted to th
but they had confidence in
and her benevolence.

They desired to be fed. S
hundreds a few years bef
and famine.

Eventually the Commiss
asked this to be reduced
they asked time to consid
ed. When the conference r
counter-proposal. This the
gave full and definite ansv

e carefully interpreted, two
Christie and McKay, being
watching how the answers
when necessary. The food
romise, that in the event of
such aid as the Crown saw
d that for three years after
rovisions to the extent of
ted them during seed-time.
s to those of the previous
evised proposals. The trea-
ully, and was then signed,
dance therewith. After the
mmissioners were unwill-
d remain out of the treaty,
essenger, Pierre Levailler,
ay, at the camp of the Hon.
e opportunity of accepting
concluded. The letter was
Rev. Père André, a Catholic
evailler, urged the Indians
o them, which they agreed
he Indians accordingly, at
after a full discussion, the
d head men of the Willow
ments were then made to

red to leave for Fort Pitt,
Rev. Mr. Scollan, a Catho-
t by Bishop Grandin, to be
aty, that Sweet Grass, the
, at Fort Pitt, was unaware
they despatched a messen-

ger to apprise him of them,

The Commissioners cros
neyed to Fort Pitt. Near it
Mounted Police, who convo

There they found a num
during the day, Sweet Gr
Chief and head men waited
was asked and granted bef
ference was opened. The ce
imposing. The national ste
of which a full narrative wi
ence proceeded, and the In
Carlton with the utmost g
title was extinguished in th
cept a comparatively small
comprising about 35,000 s
that the Chief Sweet Grass,
ings, met with an accidenta
by the discharge of a pisto
ties, displayed a strong de
and appealed for the aid of

The latter the Commissi
mer they were told they r
resentatives of whom wer
England, the Methodist, th
Catholic Church. The Bisho
travelled from Edmonton t
the Commissioners and as
the conclusion of the treaty
their long return journey b
at Winnipeg on the 6th day
of knowing that they had a
the efficient carrying out o

l laid the foundations of law
Valley.
y Company, the missionar-
nel McLeod of the Mounted
n, and the Half-breed popu-
to the commissioners, and

e Lieutenant-Governor, giv-
d of the negotiations attend-
arrative of the proceedings
. Jackes, Esq., M.D., Secre-
has never before been pub-
e account of the speeches of
. It is satisfactory to be able
officers of the police force
btained the adhesion to the
f the Chiefs included in the
while the head men even of
es under the provisions of

RNMENT HOUSE,
ANITOBA, *4th. December, 1876.*
nce with the request of the Privy
o negotiate the treaties which I had
Rev. George McDougall, promised
left Fort Garry on the afternoon of
ecuting my mission. I was accompa-
. Christie, and by A. G. Jackes, Esq.,
ed as my guide Mr. Pierre Levailler.
en associated in the commission, it
me at Fort Carlton.

ded the Assiniboine about five miles
hat is usually regarded as the first
ut two hundred and twenty miles.
by a party of the Sioux who have

settled on the reserve assigned to t
the greater part of the day.

I am sanguine that this settlemer
displaying a laudable industry in c
and in breaking up ground for culti
noon, but a storm coming on, I was
only travelled eight miles in all duri

On the 5th I left the Springs, and
excellent prairie, good soil, clumps
Little and Great Touchwood Hills a
South Saskatchewan, at Dumont's
on the afternoon of the 14th of Aug

Here I found over one hundred c
be ferried across the river. The sco
effects of Kis-so-wais, an enterprisi
tage la Prairie band, who at once c
of crossing.

I met, also, a young Cree who had
of welcome in the name of their nat

The reason of this step being tak
or Chippewa, from Quill Lake, in Tr
and proposed to them to unite with
river and entering the Indian coun
tain the proposal, and sent a messe

I also received from their messer
Chief Factor of the Hudson's Bay C
sioners the hospitalities of the fort.

I sent replies in advance, thankin
the kind offer of Mr. Clarke, to the e

It was late in the evening before
encamped on the heights near it.

On the morning of the 15th we le
me to announce my approaching a
from Carlton I found the Hon. Jam
by way of Fort Pelly.

Here also a Chief, Beardy of the W

He said that his people were en
were fine meadows for their horses

I was at once on my guard, and re
which was the place appointed, I w
body of them desired it.

He then asked me to stop as I pa
This I agreed to do, as I was leaving

cort me to Carlton which they did.
the men came to my carriage and
all joined in an invocation to the de-
ıad brought the Queen's messenger
emselves; one of them shook hands

king one, but as will be seen here-
l were very difficult to deal with.
at Fort Carlton, where Mr. Christie,
comfortable rooms, Mr. McKay pre-
he fort.
ık-koop, the two head Chiefs of the
to me, and welcomed me most cor-

ıat they wished the day to confer

hey desired to bring the Duck Lake

to Duck Lake to inform the Indians
ent of the Carlton Crees, about two

me that the Chief said "He had not
here except at Duck Lake, and that
on Indians, however, sent me word,
ten o'clock.
an encampment, a messenger came
g for provisions. I replied, that Mr.
of provisions, but that I would not
ısequence of the unreasonableness
uld only be given to the large en-

her with my fellow Commissioners,
ıis troop.
d been most judiciously chosen, be-
marshes and small lakes. The spot
tent overlooked the whole.
d the trees in the distance, and in
otted with clumps of wood, with the
he number of two hundred.
ed, and the Indians at once began
fire-arms, singing and dancing. In
ance and meet me. This they did in
lloping in circles, shouting, singing

and discharging fire-arms.

They then performed the dance of
to the north, south, west and east, a
by the Chiefs and head men, the Indi

They then slowly advanced, the ho
approach to my tent. I advanced to me
tie and McKay, when the pipe was pr

After the stroking had been comple
council tent, satisfied that in accorda
the friendship of the Cree nation.

I then addressed the Indians in su
sent by the Queen, in compliance w
promise I had given them last year, th

I had ascertained that the Indian
they dreaded the treaty; they had be
compelled to live on the reserves who
in time of war, they would be placed i

I accordingly shaped my address,
tentions of the Government, and to
strongly on them the necessity of ch
commencing to make homes and gard
for the diminution of the buffalo and
so rapidly.

The Indians listened with great at
asked an adjournment that they migh
which was of course granted.

The Rev. C. Scollen, a Roman Cath
arrived soon after from Bow River, a
learned that Sweet Grass, the princip
ing and would not be at Fort Pitt, and
would be a great obstruction to a trea

After consulting with my colleague
him, requesting his presence, and se
the services of Mr. John McKay, of P
Rev. George McDougall on his missio

In the evening, Lieut.-Col. Jarvis
Mounted Police, and an excellent ba
private cost of one of the troops.

On the 19th, the Commissioners, e
by the band, proceeded to the Indian

The Indians again assembled, follo
the recognised leading Chiefs.

I asked them to present their Chief

from the Duck Lake Indians, asking
ıe Treaty. I replied that if the Chiefs
would have heard what I had to say,
lvance, but that the messenger could
expressed himself satisfied and took
lained to them the proposals I had to
with their present mode of living, but
them as was being done elsewhere,
was done would hold good for those

ınd on the close of my remarks Mist-
l said that "when a thing was thought
ced "this much, that we go and think

hope that the Chiefs would act wisely,

hn McKay, of the Church of England,
ich was largely attended; the Rev. Mr.

ian camp, asking that there should be
McKay agreed to do; this service was
rees.

; word that, as the previous day was
ıd wished to have the day for consul-
uesday morning. I cheerfully granted
request; but I was also aware that the
difficulty.

ınd of the few discontented Saulteaux
heir own people were either averse to
ctravagant demands. The head Chiefs
that the people should act unitedly

he time they might ask, a policy which

he Indians, when I told them that we
to hear their Chiefs.

addressed me, and asked assistance
rther help as they advanced in civili-

s of living, and that we could not feed
ttle down. The Badger, Soh-ah-moos,
when they settled, and also in case of

troubles unforeseen in the future. I
charge of their every-day life, but ir
could trust to the generosity of the

The Honourable James McKay al
mands would be understood by a
could not be granted, and explaine
Cree tongue.

At length the Indians informed n
day, but to be helped when they coı
rance how to commence, and also i
winding up the debate by stating tl
they commenced to farm, and propo
tion, and then asking for a further a

The Commissioners granted this
able, and to be ready next day with t
consider what they had said.

The whole day was occupied with
it was the turning point with regar

The Indians were, as they had bee

They saw the buffalo, the only me
were anxious to learn to support th
rant to do so, and they dreaded that
be swept off by disease or famine–al
ravages of measles, scarlet fever anc

It was impossible to listen to them
but they were very apprehensive of
put it, "a new life was dawning upor

On the 23rd the conference was r
telling them to listen and the inter
changes they desired in the terms
cow each family; an increase in the
the poor, unfortunate, blind and lan
school teachers; the exclusion of fire
ther increase in agricultural implem
freedom to cut timber on Crown la
serves before the survey; free passa
other animals, a horse, harness and
a free supply of medicines; a hand m
war they should not be liable to serv

Two spokesmen then addressed u
terms of the Treaty.

I replied to them that they had asl
promised, and that the Commission

'e, and would reply, but before doing
e of the whole people, to which the

I replied, going over their demands
r inability to grant food, and again
e did the Crown ever intervene, and
number of cattle and implements, as
e their desire to settle.
on the reserves, we would give them
to the extent of one thousand dollars
fter that time they should be able to

missionaries, though I was pleased
k to the churches, and that they saw
sent at the conference. We told them
that if they prospered they could do
e asked to fight unless they desired
n to protect their wives and children

t our modified proposals.
concluded by calling on the people,
ay so. This they all did by shouting

did not differ from his people, but
clothe their children with what was
that; he did not know how to build a

e for the Red Pheasant, Chief of the
as follows: Men to build houses for
nd head men, etc. He said what was
to cover the skin of the people, guns,
rves in a belt.
hat he was party to the requests of
t was their unanimous voice he had
ew and large demands.
ould not accede to the requests now
as they had still their old mode of

hat they accepted our offers, and the
nd remarks of Toma, and stated that
im.
Half-breeds, who wish to live on the

I explained the distinction betwe
Half-breeds who lived amongst the
sioners would consider the case of e

The treaty was then signed by m
ow-as-is and Ah-tuk-uk-koop, the h
Councillors, those signing, though
ing all the bands of any importance
Indians.

On the 24th the Commissioners
the Head Chiefs with their medals,
that Mr. Christie would give the ot
the evening.

Some half a dozen of Saulteaux t
was from Qu'Appelle, and had been
to the Carlton region. I told them th
to prevent me crossing the river anc
they were not wiser than the whol
treated with.

They did not deny the charge, an
declined to hear them further, and t
go to Fort Pitt, which I warned then

Besides these Saulteaux, there v
their proceedings, amongst them
and Pecheeto, who was the chief spo
cillor of the Fort Ellice Band.

I may mention here that the larg
Saulteaux belonged, with the Chief
Treaty Number Four, at Fort Pelly
troubling me at Fort Carlton.

Mr. Christie then commenced t
of Prince Albert, and was engaged
Amongst those paid were the few re
the Cree Chiefs as part of their band

The next morning, the 26th, the
Councillors, dressed in their unifor
farewell visit to me.

The Chiefs came forward in order
I replied briefly.

They then gave three cheers for
Mounted Police, and for Mr. Lawre
departed, firing guns as they went.

Considering it undesirable that s
the treaty, as would be the case if I l

r to them. I, therefore, prepared a
he Hon. Mr. McKay's encampment
ncampment about half way to Duck
repared then to accept the terms of
lians. My letter was entrusted to Mr.

found they had a letter written to
ept the terms of the treaty, if I came

letter to them, which was received
r urged them to accept my proposal,
Mr. Levailler to inform me that they

ners met the Willow Indians.
peeches from two of the Chiefs, I ad-
r the course they had pursued, and
em this opportunity to be included

for the people. He said some things
buffalo.
the Queen, that they were alarmed
was only one left.
,–"You have told me what you have
I accept the terms; no doubt it will
when I am utterly unable to help my-

rd to assistance that we could not
we would do would be to help them

ans the charity of the Government
importance of steps being taken to
that it would be considered by the
rth-West Territories, to see if a wise
ried out and obeyed.
n signed the treaty, and the medals
istie intimated that he was ready to

e at Duck Lake, but Mr. Christie in-
Fort Pitt, this was impossible; and
ded provisions and the clothing and
ld require to go for them.
which was at once proceeded with.
s clung to their endeavor to compel

the Commissioners to proceed to D
tion, the Chief Beardy having annou
made known to him that the treaty w

It was partly, also, owing to hosti
induce the Carlton Indians to make
land, but to lend it for four years.

The good sense and intelligence o
proposals, and the Willow Indians
the treaty.

The 29th was occupied by Mr. Chr
the clothing, and preparing for our d

An application was made to me by
the proceedings on the 23rd, to sign

As I could not ascertain that there
resident in the region to be recogni
evidence that they desired him to b
sign the treaty, but informed him t
merous enough, and expressed the
be recognized.

He was satisfied with this, and sa
payments.

His daughter, a widow, with her
main until next year, as he did not w

On the morning of the 31st, the pr
and I left for Fort Pitt, Mr. McKay ha
by way of Battle River.

We arrived on the 5th September,
our custom throughout the whole jo

About six miles from the fort we we
their band, as an escort, and also by
Bay Company, who informed us that

We found over one hundred lodge
a message from them, that as their
wished delay until the 7th.

On the morning of the 6th, Sweet
of my message, accompanied by abo
see me and express their gratificatio

Their greeting was cordial, but n
me in their arms, and kissed me on
tended also to Mr. Christie and Dr. J

The Hon. James McKay arrived fr
ported that he had met there a numb
had been camped there for some time

poorer Indians had gone after them.
hey would like to have waited until
ere, to see me and accept the treaty,
consequence to them that they could

Crees and Saulteaux from Jack Fish

led to the council tent, which was
t, commanding a very fine view, and

the police, with their band.
p and ceremony, following the lead

t Carlton, but with much more cere-
one, and the number of riders, sing-
After the pipes were stroked by the
each of them to be smoked, and then
lico and cloth, and returned to their

s I addressed them, telling them we
there was now a trail leading from
it stretching on thence to Fort Elli-
ck going to Qu'Appelle and Cypress
ton, and thence I expected to see it
ky Mountains; on that road I saw all
saw along it gardens being planted

ns and walk with the white men on
t Carlton, and offered them the same
wished it.
me by the hand, asked me to explain
would all shake hands with me and

d the terms fully to them, both ad-
ours. On concluding they expressed

ne to deliberate, which was granted,
to make exorbitant demands, and we
the avenues by which we had access

d to the council tent, but the Indians
ncil, endeavoring to agree amongst

At length they approached and se
asked them to speak to me. The Ea
to be afraid, and that I was to them
to establish was for their good.

After some time had passed, I ag
and not to be afraid. Sweet Grass t
sible manner. He thanked the Qu
a brother and a friend who would
condition. He thanked me for the
therefore accepted gladly, and too
looking down on us that day, and
Grass further said, he pitied those
if spared until this time next year,
ernor), to commence to act for hir
would commence at once to prepa
would do the same.

Placing one hand over my heart,
the white man's blood never be s
white man and red man can stand t
your heart, let us be as one; use yo
so that they may prosper."

The Chief's speech, of which the
words, was assented to by the peo
takes with them the place of the Br

I replied, expressing my satisfa
proved of the arrangement I had m
ised that I would send them next y
copies of the treaty printed on parc

I said that I knew that some of t
would receive the present of money

The Commissioners then signed
Chiefs and those of their Councillor
me before signing. James Senum, (
that he commenced to cultivate the

Mr. Christie, then chief factor o
plough, but it was now broken. He
and his people drew the plough th
Mr. Christie also gave him a pit-sav
them. His heart was sore in spring
had no implements. He asked for t
the Wesleyan mission at that plac
taught it helps me a great deal.

The Little Hunter, a leading Chie

ıor's hand as if it was the Queen's.
put this country to rights, it is the
vished an everlasting grasp of her
ıo would prosper. All the children
reat Spirit would look down upon
ves similarly.
ayan or mountaineer, a small band

had selected a Chief and presented
, that he thanked the Queen, and
at had been done, and if he could
aid more.
niform, and flag, the band playing
ising to their feet.
s, were distributed, as soon as pos-
e the payments.
onducted the service for the police
afternoon the Rev. Mr. McDougall
the Rev. Mr. Scollen also had ser-

ted the payments and distribution
ing the Saskatchewan, with a view
River. We therefore sent our horses
nts pitched with the view of com-
morning. Just as we were about
, one of the three Cree Chiefs who
to see me. The Commissioners met
on the plains hunting the buffalo,
; that on hearing of it he had been
Assiniboines to speak for them. I
rlton and Pitt, he expressed regret
k to me. I then said we would not
him much.
Chiefs and Councillors came down
rewell.
t. The Bear said the Indians on the
d those who were away were as a

e the representative of the Queen
eir hearts to come to our help. Let
culty that this was brought about.
ı spoke similarly.
saw the Governor before; when I

heard he was to come, I said I will
dread–hanging; it was not given to
replied, that God had given it to us
the protection the police force affor
Big Bear still demanded that the
him that his request would not be
might be protected, and asked why
The Fish, the Chippewayan repli
spoken, and what he says we all say
I then asked the Bear to tell the ot
amat, what had been done; that I ha
it by Sweet Grass, and that next ye
to the buffalo, the North-West Cour
again explained that we would not i
to assist them in farming.
I then said I never expected to se
another Governor was to be sent, w
had done me, and give him the same
Chiefs and Councillors, commenci
with Mr. Christie and myself, each a
The Bear remained sitting until
and holding it, said, "If he had kn
people. I am not an undutiful child,
people are not here I do not sign. I
year I will come." The Indians then
to see me again, fearing I had not f
he accepted the treaty as if he had
all his people and accept it.
We crossed the river, and left for
arrived on the afternoon of the 15t
Pheasant and his band, whom we h
On the 16th, the Red Pheasant s
Battle River Indian; his fathers had
see the Government coming there, a
wished the claims of the Half-breed
ment came to be respected, as for hi
home, and though it was hard to le
make way for the white man, and su
the Queen, when she hears of this,
should be given him to plant potato
after digging them, to their reserve
at the Eagle Hills.
I expressed my satisfaction with

ɔf the Pacific telegraph line, who is
ıat the band should use three acres
moreover, Mr. Fuller kindly prom-

ur camp, and on Monday morning,
ourney, with the incidents of which
ıte that, on arriving on the 4th of
miles from Portage la Prairie, we
carts to follow us leisurely (many
exhausted with the long journey of
ıe Portage; on the 5th we reached
ıckes remained, their horses being
lar Point, forty-five miles from Fort
he night from Mr. Chisholm, of the

of the 6th of October having been
McKay, having taken another road,
Jackes reached here subsequently.
roceedings, I proceed to deal with
for your consideration some reflec-
ons.

ritory are chiefly Crees, but there
also at the slope of the mountains.
x and one band of Chippewayans.
great a willingness on the part of
, and so great a desire to have their
stie to confer with the Chief while
alities where they would desire to
few exceptions they indicated the
ommenced to settle.
ıd agricultural implements should

ion should be made for forwarding
it probable that cattle and some im-
ɔert and thus avoid transportation.
gh I did not grant the request, I
ıstructed in farming and building,
ommend that measures be adopted
r present mode of living is passing
willing to learn. I think that advan-
teach them to become self-support-
the aid of a few practical farmers
g and house building.

The universal demand for teache
aries, is also encouraging. The for
latter they must rely on the church
extend their operations amongst t
the cry of the Indian for help is a cl

4th. In connection with the aidir
tention to the necessity of regulatio
buffalo. These animals are fast decr
a few simple regulations would pre
ject was constantly pressed on my
that the matter would be considere
that has governed the territories f
turing a law for this purpose, and
passed a statute for their preservati
of our successors as one of urgent

5th. There is another class of th
sition I desire to bring under the
wandering Half-breeds of the plair
live the life of the Indians. There ar
but there is a large class of Metis w
no settled homes. I think that a cen
cured, and while I would not be di
under the treaties, I would suggest
that on their settling down, if after
it should be found necessary and e
them to enable them to enter upon

If the measures suggested by n
with regard to the buffalo, the Inc
erratic Half-breeds encouraged to
all social questions of any present
will have been arrived at.

In conclusion, I have to call your
Hon. Mr. Christie, which I forward
charge of the payments and admi
treaty, and I have to speak in the hi

Accompanying his report will be
tribution of provisions and clothir
reserves, suggestions as to the tim
general balance sheet.

A credit of $60,000 was given tc
credit of the Receiver-General, $12
ing to the proximity of the buffalc
the treaty.

from the services of the Hon.
dian encampment. He had the
learning their views which his
n to do. Dr. Jackes took a warm
; a record of the negotiations, a
ht to be published, as it will be
administer the treaty, showing
nd by the Indians, and prevent-
mmissioners are under obliga-
officers and men of the police

he presence of the force as an
uthority in the North-West was

ness of Messrs. Clarke, of Fort
other officials of the Hudson's
y extended towards the accom-
on the interest taken in the ne-
nd by the various missionaries,

Half-breed population whether
nce of their relationship to the
satisfactory arrangement with

rs, having secured the services
while the Indians had engaged
. The latter acted as chief inter-
nost efficient interpreter.
have only in conclusion to ex-
gress of the work of the Domin-
ficial to them, and of advantage

e, Sir,
t servant,
EXANDER MORRIS,
Lieut.-Governor.

PART THREE

A FEELING VEILED VERY GENERALLY
A LYING IN THE UNCEDED

V

The long weeks of rain have made the creek run high. The island I visit is flooded. As a science student I collected invertebrates from this island in early mornings of an autumn years ago. The still pool of bright red sediment has rejoined the Whitemud in full. The rapids are nearly loud enough to drown the freeway noise from outside the valley. The afternoon heat bakes with a soothing humidity of leaves growing and transpiring water. Green broken by more green broken by silver broken by brown and red and yellow.

RELEVANT FACTS AND NUMERALS OF TREATY AND MÉTIS SCRIP

The gold border is 3 mm from the edges of the front cover, with the exception of the left-hand side of the cover which is 7 mm from the binding edge.

However, because the binding is missing,
it is impossible to say exactly how far from the edge this gold border would have been.

The gold border itself is 1mm wide.

EDMONTON CITY PLANNING: 1890–2022

The McKernan and Parkallen lakes were places that people gathered, fished, and performed ceremony.

The lakes were surveyed within the lands of the Papaschase reserve. The reserve was extinguished through fraud. Settler squatters of the city of Strathcona claimed the land before its eventual annexation by Edmonton.

They drained the lakes to make room for more homesteads.

But the ground remembers, and occasionally still floods in times of heavy rains.

A NATURAL YARD IS NOT

Support local wildlife in this section. Incorporate native, drought-resistant plants. Over-watering is a waste of water. A natural yard is inspired. A natural yard is inspired to create interest and use rocks. Create interest. Use rocks. A natural yard emphasizes native plant species. Opt for native and drought-resistant plants. You may trap pest animals on your own property. In some cases just leave them alone. On your property: skunks, gophers, porcupines, squirrels, ground squirrels, magpies, crows. Click here to rent traps from the city. The city no longer offers trap rental services. Offering traps is a non-legislated and non-traditional municipal activity. Traps can pose a significant risk of injury to citizens and animals. Porcupines require large cage traps. Rated porcupine size. These will be very large. Set traps in areas of high porcupine activity. Bait with salted apple slices. Place a small dish of freshwater in the trap. Over-watering is a waste of water. Check the trap frequently. Relocate any trapped porcupine at least fifteen kilometres from capture site. Relocating may cause difficulty. Quills typically lie flat until a porcupine is threatened. There are pest control businesses. Look for them in the Yellow Pages under exterminators. We offer a year-round insect identification service. Send specimens through the mail. During the summer months, magpies eat a considerable number of insects. Magpies are a common winter resident in central and southern Alberta. Migration may occur in varying degrees. Magpies followed the buffalo here. Magpies need the increased food supplies that human settlement brings. You may trap pest animals on your own property such as magpies. It seems a paradox that one of the most clever and most beautiful could also be a serious pest. Allow birds to become accustomed to the trap. Entice the birds to enter. Note: the above operations should be carried out late in the day to avoid disturbing the routine of the magpies.

EDMONTON
HUDSON'S BAY COMPANY'S RESERVE
Government Property
H.B.CO.
Brick Yard
Packing Plant
Golf Links
CITY PARK
Coal Mine
Clays
Packing Plant
UNIVERSITY
R. LOT 7
CITY PARK
PACKING PLANT
Canadian Pacific Railway Property
STRATHCONA

CHAPTER IX.

THE TREATIES AT FORTS CARLTON AND PITT.

The treaties made at Forts Carlton and Pitt in the year 1876, were of a very important character.

The great region covered by them, abutting on the areas ncluded in Treaties Numbers Three and Four, embracing n area of approximately 120,000 square miles, contains a ast extent of fertile territory and is the home of the Cree ation. The Crees had, very early after the annexation of the orth-West Territories to Canada, desired a treaty of allince with the Government. So far back as the year 1871, Mr. impson, the Indian Commissioner, addressing the Secreary of State in a despatch of date, the 3rd November, 1871, sed the following language:

"I desire also to call the attention of His Excellency to the tate of affairs in the Indian country on the Saskatchewan. he intelligence that Her Majesty is treating with the Chipewa Indians has already reached the ears of the Cree and lackfeet tribes. In the neighborhood of Fort Edmonton, on he Saskatchewan, there is a rapidly increasing population f miners and other white people, and it is the opinion of Mr. W. J. Christie, the officer in charge of the Saskatchewan istrict, that a treaty with the Indians of that country, or at east an assurance during the coming year that a treaty will hortly be made, is essential to the peace, if not the actual re-

Messages from the Cree Chiefs of the Plains, Saskatchewan, to His Ex
cy Governor Archibald, our Great Mother's representative at Fort Ga
d River Settlement.

The Chief Sweet Grass, The Chief of the country.

GREAT FATHER,–I shake hands with you, and bid you welcome. We he
r lands were sold and we did not like it; we don't want to sell our lands; i
r property, and no one has a right to sell them.

Our country is getting ruined of fur-bearing animals, hitherto our sole s
rt, and now we are poor and want help–we want you to pity us. We w
ttle, tools, agricultural implements, and assistance in everything when
me to settle–our country is no longer able to support us.

Make provision for us against years of starvation. We have had great s
tion the past winter, and the small-pox took away many of our people,
l, young, and children.

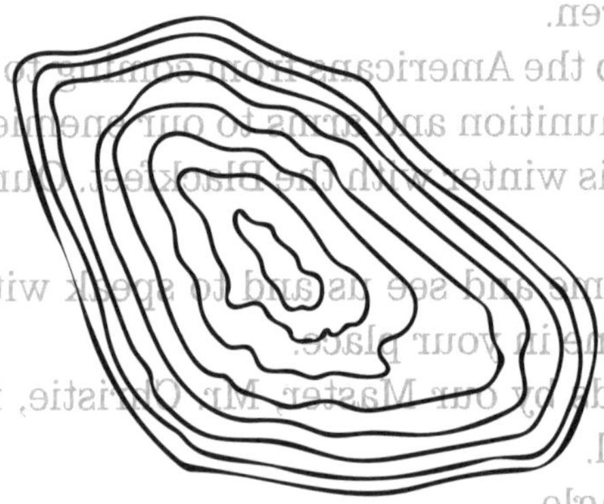

We want you to stop the Americans from coming to trade on our lands, a
ving firewater, ammunition and arms to our enemies the Blackfeet.

We made a peace this winter with the Blackfeet. Our young men are fooli
may not last long.

We invite you to come and see us and to speak with us. If you can't co
urself, send some one in your place.

We send these words by our Master, Mr. Christie, in whom we have ev
nfidence.–That is all.

Ki-he-win, The Eagle.

GREAT FATHER,–Let us be friendly. We never shed any white man's blo
d have always been friendly with the whites, and want workmen, carp
's and farmers to assist us when we settle. I want all my brother, Sw
ass, asks. That is all.

The Little Hunter.

You, my brother, the Great Chief in Red River, treat me as a brother; t
as a Great Chief.

Kis-ki-on, or Short Tail.

My brother, that is coming close, I look upon you, as if I saw you; I w
u to pity me, and I want help to cultivate the ground for myself and desc
nts. Come and see us.

The North-West Council, as already elsewhere stated, h
rged the making of treaties with these Indians, and t
ecessity of doing so, was also impressed upon the Pri
ouncil, by the Lieutenant-Governor of the North-West T

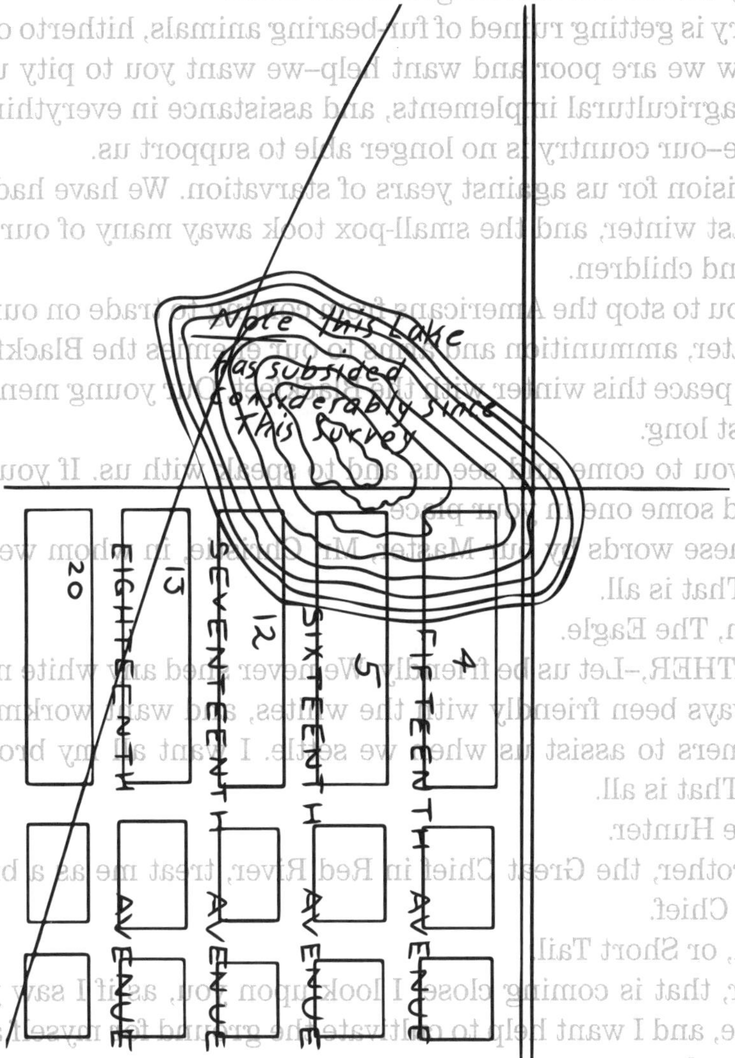
Note this Lake
has subsided
considerably since
this survey
20
13
12
5
4
EIGHTEENTH AVENUE
SEVENTEENTH AVENUE
SIXTEENTH AVENUE
FIFTEENTH AVENUE

VI

Sitting on a driftwood log beside the rapids, I think about how this place is in the holdings of the university and how it holds a part-whole relationship to the artificial construct that is higher learning. I think about how this is an inversion of the part-whole relationship that the university has with the landscape it is in. I think that this steep-sided valley is my most important lecture theatre. This is where I learn how to live, with myself and with what I know, with my relations in the water, on the land, in the air.

RELEVANT FACTS AND NUMERALS OF TREATY AND MÉTIS SCRIP

The gold 'Department of Indian Affairs' text is 17 mm from the bottom edge of the front cover. It is 66 mm wide.

'Indian' is 13 mm wide.
'Affairs' is 11 mm wide.
'Department' is mostly missing.

The capital letters and ascenders (A, f, d, etc.) are 4 mm high. The lower-case letters with no ascenders (s, a, etc.) are a hair over 2 mm high.

We heard
our lands were sold
and no one has a right to sell them.

Note this Lake

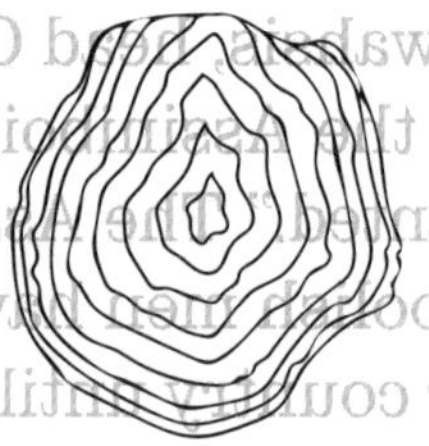

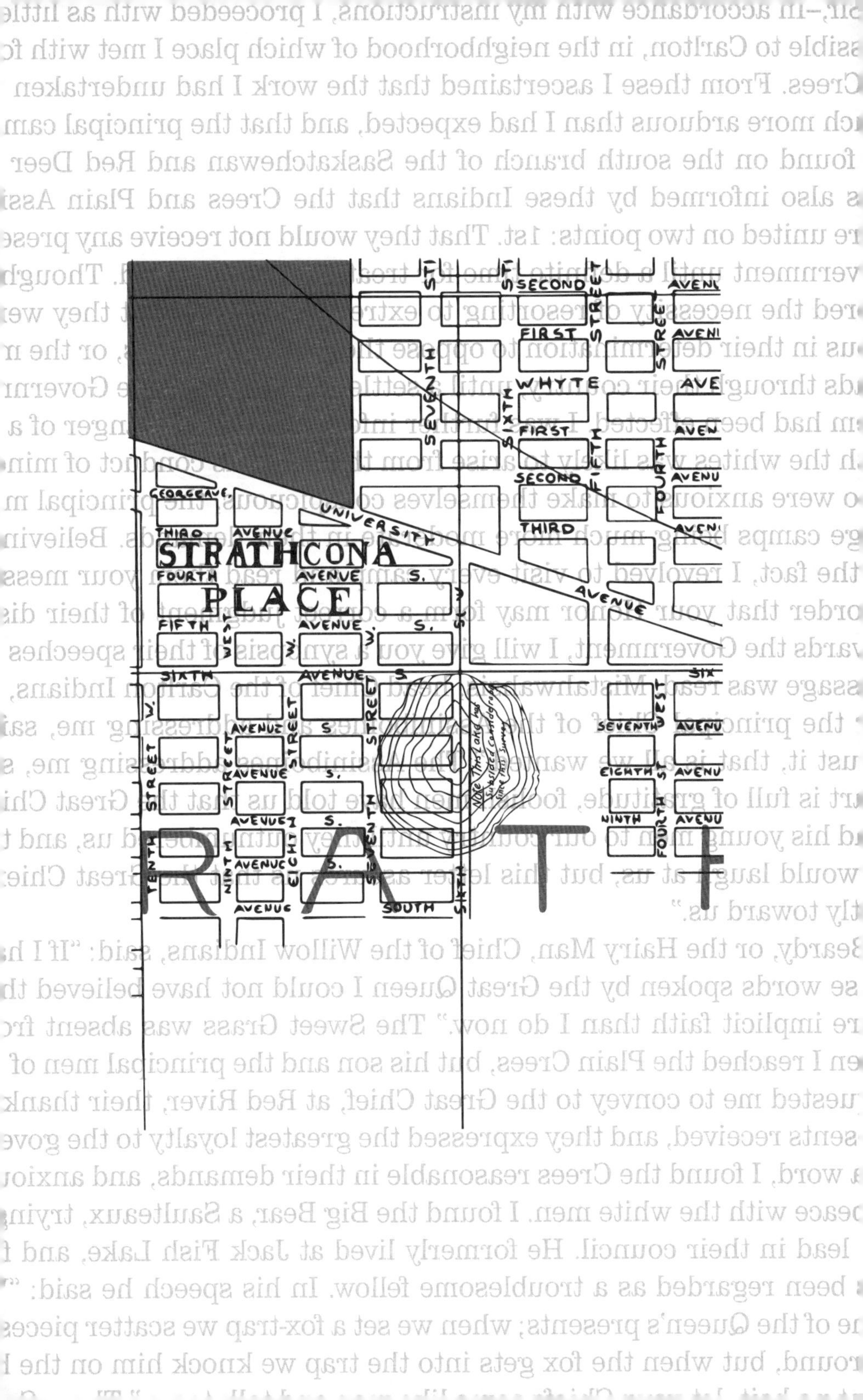
STRATHCONA
PLACE
UNIVERSITY
AVENUE
GEORGE AVE.
THIRD AVENUE
FOURTH AVENUE
FIFTH AVENUE
SIXTH AVENUE S
AVENUE S.
EIGHTH AVENUE
NINTH AVENUE
AVENUE
SOUTH
SECOND AVENUE
FIRST AVENUE
WHYTE AVE
FIRST AVENUE
SECOND AVENUE
THIRD AVENUE
SEVENTH AVENUE
TENTH STREET W.
NINTH STREET
EIGHTH STREET
SEVENTH STREET
SIXTH ST
SEVENTH
SIXTH
FIFTH STREET
FOURTH STREET
FOURTH ST WEST
Note This Lake has subsided considerably since this Survey
RATT

VII

My presence calls mosquitos to me in a cloud. For the mosquitos, blood makes me a patch of resources in the landscape. Orbiting this cloud are dragonflies hunting mosquitos for food. They dive into the cloud to intercept the mosquitos in the air. For the dragonflies, mosquitos make me a patch of resources in the landscape. These insects both have aquatic larval life stages. They are born in the water. They meet again in the air around me. I belong to the land.

I am grateful for being a part of these relations.

RELEVANT FACTS AND NUMERALS OF TREATY AND MÉTIS SCRIP

The spacing between 'TREATY' and 'NUMBER ELEVEN' is 17 mm from the bottom line of 'TREATY' to the top line of 'NUMBER ELEVEN.' The 'N' of 'NUMBER' is 94 mm from the left hand edge of the front cover. The 'N' of 'ELEVEN' is 92 mm from the right hand edge of the front cover. The topline of 'NUMBER' is 152 mm from the top edge of the front cover. The bottom line of 'ELEVEN' is 186 mm from the bottom edge of the front cover.

'TREATY' is 83 mm wide.
'NUMBER ELEVEN' is 104 mm.
'NUMBER' is 50 mm.
'ELEVEN' is 47 mm wide.

The capital letters are approximately 11 mm tall.
'NUMBER ELEVEN' letter 'E's are 6 mm wide.
TREATY letter Es are 9 mm wide.

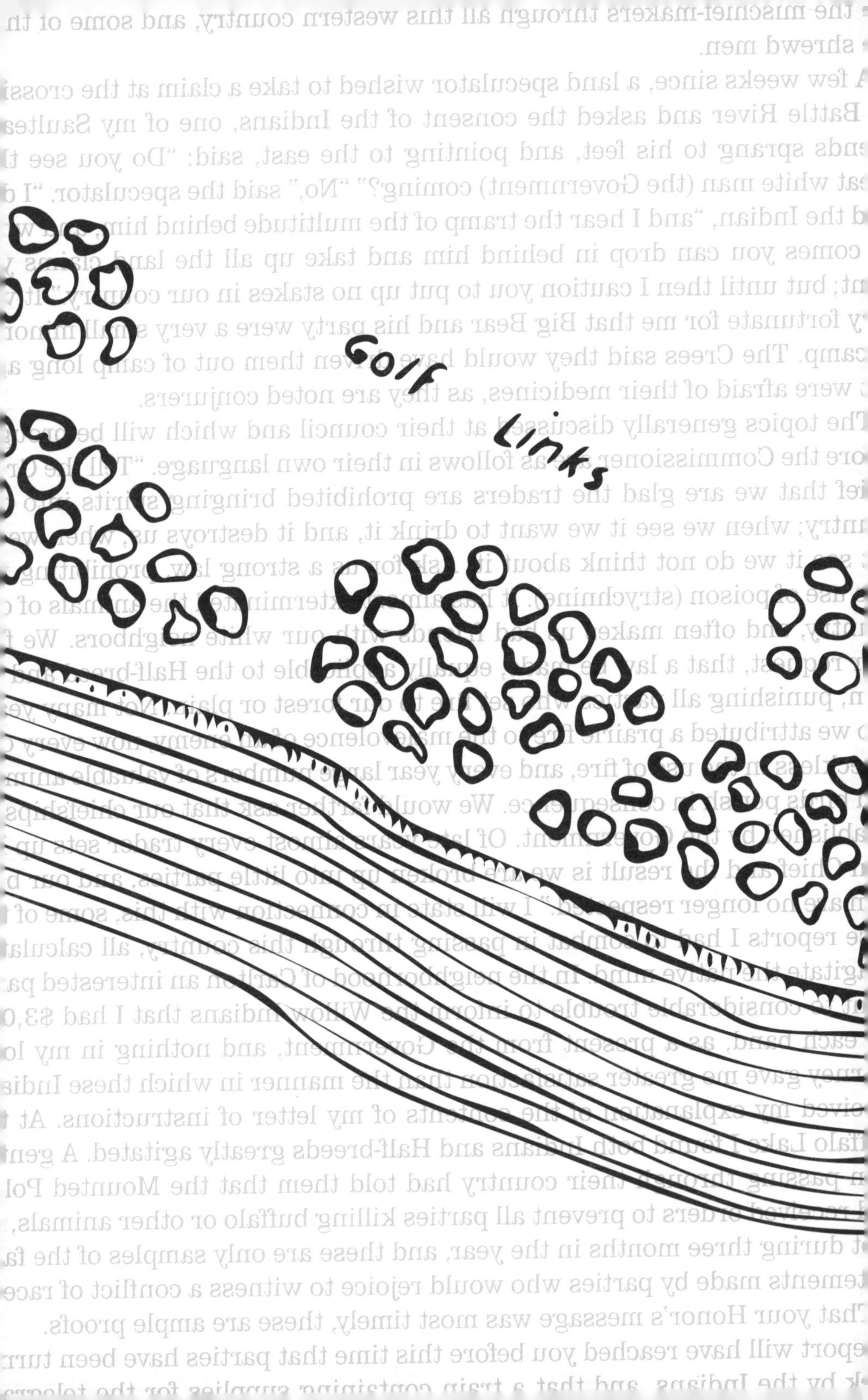
Golf Links

ments of all parties concerned, my opinion is, that an old traveller amongst Indians would have regarded the whole affair as too trivial to be noticed. I have not met with a Chief who would bear with the responsibility of the act....

Personally I am indebted both to the missionaries, and the Hudson's Bay Company's officials for their assistance at the Indian councils.

Believing it would be satisfactory to your Honor and of service to the Commissioners, I have kept the number of all the tents visited and the names of the places where I met the Indians.

By reckoning eight persons to each tent, we will have a very close approximate to the number of Indians to be treated with at Carlton, and Fort Pitt. There may have been a few tents in the forest, and I have heard there are a few Crees at Lesser Slave Lake and Lac la Biche, but the number cannot exceed twenty tents.

All of which is respectfully submitted.

G. McDOUGALL.

The Commissioners, in the discharge of their task, had to travel through the prairie district in going to their destination and returning to Winnipeg, a distance of over 1,800 miles. They first met the Indians in the vicinity of Fort Carlton, on the Saskatchewan, in the month of August, 1876, and eventually succeeded on the 23rd of that month, in effecting a treaty with the Plain and Wood Crees, and on the 28th of the same month with the tribe of Willow Crees. The negotiations were difficult and protracted. The Hon. David Mills, then Minister of the Interior, in his Annual Report thus characterizes them: "In view of the temper of the Indians of the Saskatchewan, during the past year, and of the extravagant demands which they were induced to prefer on certain points, it needed all the temper, tact, judgment and discretion, of which the Commissioners were possessed, to bring the negotiations to a satisfactory issue."

r e l a t iv e s ab u n d a n c e

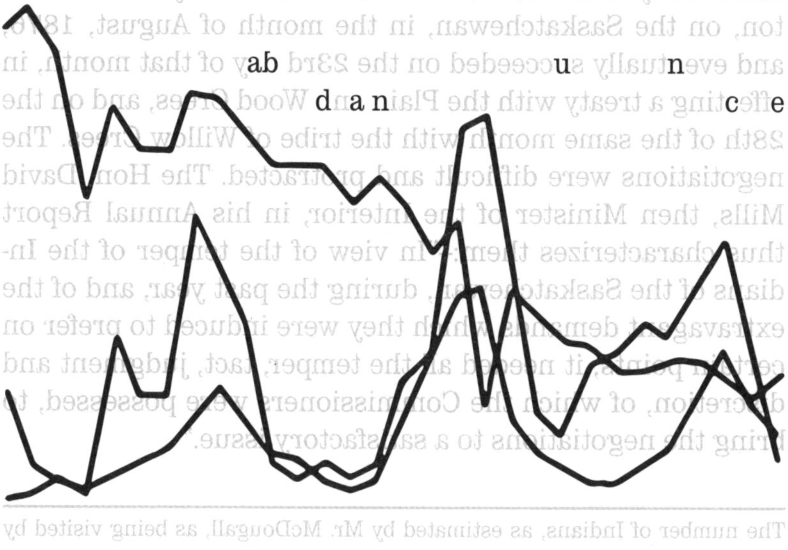

The number of Indians, as estimated by Mr. McDougall, as being visited by him, was 3,976.

URBAN FOREST MANAGEMENT PLAN

Found book. Unbound. Edges cut square. Each square numbered, towned. Lilac corners. Caragana-hedged edges. Historical-board old. Urban elm forest. City on the river banks. Here among majestic planted trees, green carpets of seeded lawn, flowering imported shrubs and invasive plants, the countryside is painted with both breath and taking beauty. Historical-board old. See this graph. The urban forest is one of the city's greatest assets. It refineries our air and redistributes the water from our drained gathering lakes. It creates a new environment with gentrified, static, and picture-frame neighbourhoods the mayor can be proud of, committed to, ensured of its long-term maintenance and growth. Historical-board old. The city has recognized the value of integrating the natural environment with an urban landscape. All crowded populations call for sustainable life in healthy green spaces and happy natural areas. The beauty of nature is peaceful. The city is sordid. Although home to a wide range of tree species, relatively few are native to the region. Early settlers encountered a prairie landscape. Aspen, poplar, birch, and spruce. The transformation to the diverse urban forest found today has been a long-term effort so wonderfully refreshing to the tired souls of city dwellers and artificial city lives. Open spaces to be used when necessity requires by citizens. Created boulevards and planted trees to beautify growth, benefit residents, attract newcomers. To make us love our city, we must make our city lovely. Make us love our city. Make our city lovely. Historical-board old. Blessed in natural beauty requiring united efforts of those who guide her destinies. Our city. Historical-board old. The city partners develop business and citizens continue to expand our range of tree species. A value appreciating over time.

Police therein. The Min
Mills, in his Report for
subject:

"Official reports rece
ernor Morris and Colo
mand of the Mounted P
showed that a feeling
vailed very generally a
lying in the unceded t
and the Rocky Mounta
prevailed amongst the
been increased by the p
tory of the parties eng
graph line, and in the s
also of a party belongi
this state of feeling, a
ty of the Indian tribes
Government, His Honc
tained authority to des
Indians the assurance
this summer, to negoti
been done with their b

"The Rev. George M
a missionary amongs
teen years, and who p
was selected by His H
Indians, a task which
success: being able to
he found the feeling
among the Indian tri
remove it by his ass
during the coming ye

"For the purpose of

The view was very beautiful:

On my arrival, the Union Jack was hoisted

DOMINION LAND SURVEY

'The land system in western Canada was based on a unique checkerboard survey developed for the Prairies by the Canadian government. This system covered 200 million acres and is the world's largest survey grid laid down in a single integrated system. It led to the creation of more than 1.25 million homesteads.'

– Description of the Western Canada land system, *Land Grants of Western Canada, 1870–1930*

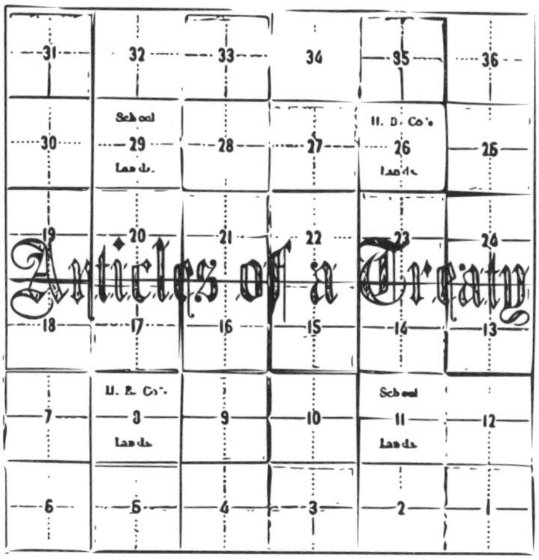

VIII

There is a patience I seem to have only when staring at water. I feel as though I could wait long enough for the creek to repeat itself.

RELEVANT FACTS AND NUMERALS OF TREATY AND MÉTIS SCRIP

' ... it was not their fault that the treaty had not been made in 1921, as they were there awaiting your representative who failed to put in an appearance.'

– Thomas Harris, Indian Agent at Fort Simpson

The Treaty Commission had planned to meet signatories at Liard in the summer of 1921. Notices had been issued requesting the presence of signatories. Due to high water and the difficulties of travel, which were made clear to the Commission party only upon its intended departure from Edmonton, Liard was not reached during the 1921 signings.

WHAT THE CROWN PREPARED BUT DID NOT BRING TO LIARD

Signed at **Liard** on the .... day of .... 1921, by His Majesty's Commissioner and the Chiefs and Headmen in the Presence of the Undersigned Witnesses, after having been first interpreted and explained.

Witnesses:

....

....

....

....

EDMONTON'S WHITEMUD CREEK

They used the white mud
of the creek
to whitewash the buildings
of the fort.

J.A.R. Balsillie

1921: TREATY NO. 11

My lungs are full of spruce trees
but otherwise I am empty,
I am here to witness:

1921,
and Grandfather is working for the Company in Fort Providence.
It is June, and that far north
the sun would not set on the British Empire.

He signs the treaty with a heavy ink.

Dreamt I was a library again,
it is an all-or-nothing calling.
I have language for it,
I have bones
but otherwise am formless before the 7am alarm
held loose on birdsong, briefly,
between the low notes on their way to the water.

I am bounded by the geese,
and punctuated by the dwindling of the caribou.

2020: WITNESS (CONTINUED)

Dreamt I was a river again,
a thread of a glacier unwinding itself in slow motion,
slow enough to dip hands in and drink.

‘I wish to be treated the same as other people have been treated.’

– J. A. R. Balsillie,
from his application
for Métis scrip

IX

How the wind catching one stand of grass appears to move through to another stand of grass. How the wind, which is a changing of pressures, seems to travel as the sun heats different parts of the atmosphere at once. How the plants seem to travel as the sun shines on different parts of the ground at once. How the animals seem to travel as the plants grow on different parts of the ground at once. How the water across the ground seems to travel as the atmosphere and the plants and the animals move across the ground in different ways at once.

RELEVANT FACTS AND NUMERALS OF TREATY AND MÉTIS SCRIP

Marie Fabien's Half-Breed Scrip was defrauded from her by thieves in Edmonton in 1907.

No. A12759 for $160.00.
No. A4390 for $80.00.

My great-great grandmother spent twenty-seven years of her life trying to set right this injustice. Twenty-seven years of waiting for the gears of the government to turn in her favour.

Despite the Halfbreed Commissioner petitioning on her behalf, the Deputy Minister of the Interior and Controller for the Land Patents Branch repeatedly denied her claim.

Two of the thieves falsley claimed to witness Marie's signature:

Walter Taylor
James Brewster

The other thieves included the Edmonton law firm of Short, Cross, Biggar, and Ewing, who participated in the fraud, writing repeatedly to the department over a course of years. They attempted to exchange this defrauded scrip for land parcels. The request was denied, and cash was given to them instead.

The lawyer Charles Cross was Alberta's Attorney-General at the time. He resigned along with the province's Premier, Alexander Rutherford, over campaign bribes and a railway scandal.

THE CPR WANTED TO PROVE THE PARALLEL LINE THEOREM

I

Theorem #1:

The Parallel Line Theorem

Two lines are parallel if and only if the corresponding angles of a line that crosses those two lines, are equal.

Proof Method #1:

Mathematical Induction

A form of proof whereby proving both the basic case (n) and demonstrating the ability to prove subsequent cases (n+1) from the base results in a proof of all subsequent cases (n = 0, 1, 2, 3, ...).

Proof Method #2:

Proof by Exhaustion

A form of proof whereby all cases (n = 0, 1, 2, 3, ...) are proven individually.

Also called the 'brute force' method.

II

In some ways, proof is a thing that belongs on the landscape. In the language of logical systems, agreement between two things is a form of argument. The CPR could never prove things through mathematical induction. It was too difficult to make the move from proving one thing to proving everything that came after. Mathematical induction was also difficult because it was not profitable. Paper and ink could not transport silver or other elements of the mountains. Exhaustion would be the way forward.

III

For the federal government, it was in the national interest to prove things by train. The national endeavour, argued Macdonald, would be in this new kind of mathematics. A mathematics that everyone could understand, because of how loud it would be, and because the transportation of dangerous goods through small towns would result in magnificent destruction.

IV

The new math would bring tourists from the old country, some might even stay. It would also be a dramatic method for killing grizzly bears. The train would be useful for bisecting planes of habitat in general. This would be a useful technique when working on other geometric theorems in the future, like the Dominion land survey, and war.

V

Postulates of iron were placed congruent with the land. These postulates were crossed individually with one line after the other. With each line, the proof became more rigorous and the rail became more useful. Exhaustion occurred in those that stretched the proof beyond the realm of paper and ink. But no matter how many lines were crossed, there were still more to go. Eventually the lines reached the mountains. The CPR was certain of its brute force method. The federal government continued to pledge its support.

VI

Scandal and bribery had collapsed earlier attempts at the proof, but Macdonald's second government was resilient in the face of exhaustion.

VII

Power and ability and movement and stability the railway proved along.

VIII

When Lord Strathcona drove the last spike into the Rocky Mountains, it was a splitting of the atom. In these parallel lines lay the power of empire.

IX

The land was now accessible without the need to touch it. People and places were connected by being separated.

X

The proof was complete. New assumptions were now commonplace and available for use by the public with purchase:

the land was empty –
the land was available –
the land was ready –

passage money advanced. Loans for farm purchase. Apply within. The CPR assumed a role of pressure such that speaking of it changing was a speaking into being of storms.

THE BUREAU OF CANADIAN INFORMATION
DEPT. OF COLONIZATION & DEVELOPMENT
CANADIAN PACIFIC RAILWAY

1872: PRIME MINISTER MACDONALD ASKS FOR A BRIBE

With less than a week before the election, the Prime Minister,
Sir John A. Macdonald,
sends a telegram to the lawyer of Hugh Allan, railway financier:

I MUST HAVE ANOTHER $10,000.
WILL BE THE LAST TIME OF CALLING. DO NOT FAIL ME.
ANSWER TODAY.

1873: PRIME MINISTER MACDONALD TESTIFIES ON BRIBERY ALLEGATIONS

The Prime Minister Sir John A. Macdonald
was deposed on September 17, 1873:

Question – The second sum of money received by you, of $10,000, was in consequence, I think, of a telegram which has appeared?

Answer – I would not like to swear that I sent exactly that telegram, because I do not remember its terms, but I sent a telegram, and I have no doubt that this is the telegram.

1885: BOUND IN IRON

Men pose in unceded Secwepemc territory.

Lord Strathcona is pictured hammering metal into the earth. Strathcona was the namesake of the city in which I was born, one century after this photo was taken.

Not pictured here are the Canadian soldiers sent by rail to attack the Métis and the provisional government of Saskatchewan. The resistance against this violence would end in the displacement of Métis across the North-West, including from the city in which I was born. Strathcona notoriously profited from this violence through land speculation in the systemic fraud of Métis scrip.

This photograph would become perhaps the most famous photograph in Canada's history. Early historians suggested a copy of it should be placed in each school room in the nation.

WHERE THE TRACK MEETS THE TRAIL OUTSIDE MY DOOR TO PÊHONÂN

There is nothing the train hates more than derailment.
To be on track and moving,
and moving off track.

A derailment is a spilling of very tightly wound expectation.
It is a screeching at the frequency of no brakes.

I think about that photo of Lord Strathcona a lot
and how if you press your ear to the steel here down the road
the steel that says the gauge is:
OH - CANADA

you can hear the old thief tapping with his hammer.

CPR ADVERTISEMENTS OF A POPULATED LANDSCAPE

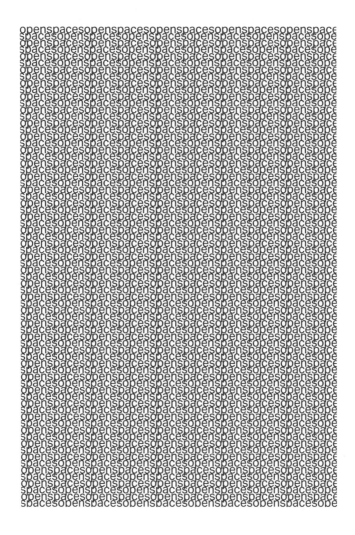

openspacesopenspacesopenspacesopenspacesopenspace
spacesopenspacesopenspacesopenspacesopenspacesope
openspacesopenspacesopenspacesopenspacesopenspace
spacesopenspacesopenspacesopenspacesopenspacesope
openspacesopenspacesopenspacesopenspacesopenspace
spacesopenspacesopenspacesopenspacesopenspacesope
openspacesopenspacesopenspacesopenspacesopenspace
spacesopenspacesopenspacesopenspacesopenspacesope
openspacesopenspacesopenspacesopenspacesopenspace
spacesopenspacesopenspacesopenspacesopenspacesope
openspacesopenspacesopenspacesopenspacesopenspace
spacesopenspacesopenspacesopenspacesopenspacesope
openspacesopenspacesopenspacesopenspacesopenspace
spacesopenspacesopenspacesopenspacesopenspacesope
openspacesopenspacesopenspacesopenspacesopenspace
spacesopenspacesopenspacesopenspacesopenspacesope
openspacesopenspacesopenspacesopenspacesopenspace
spacesopenspacesopenspacesopenspacesopenspacesope
openspacesopenspacesopenspacesopenspacesopenspace
spacesopenspacesopenspacesopenspacesopenspacesope
openspacesopenspacesopenspacesopenspacesopenspace
spacesopenspacesopenspacesopenspacesopenspacesope
openspacesopenspacesopenspacesopenspacesopenspace
spacesopenspacesopenspacesopenspacesopenspacesope
openspacesopenspacesopenspacesopenspacesopenspace
spacesopenspacesopenspacesopenspacesopenspacesope
openspacesopenspacesopenspacesopenspacesopenspace
spacesopenspacesopenspacesopenspacesopenspacesope
openspacesopenspacesopenspacesopenspacesopenspace
spacesopenspacesopenspacesopenspacesopenspacesope
openspacesopenspacesopenspacesopenspacesopenspace
spacesopenspacesopenspacesopenspacesopenspacesope
openspacesopenspacesopenspacesopenspacesopenspace
spacesopenspacesopenspacesopenspacesopenspacesope
openspacesopenspacesopenspacesopenspacesopenspace
spacesopenspacesopenspacesopenspacesopenspacesope
openspacesopenspacesopenspacesopenspacesopenspace
spacesopenspacesopenspacesopenspacesopenspacesope
openspacesopenspacesopenspacesopenspacesopenspace
spacesopenspacesopenspacesopenspacesopenspacesope
openspacesopenspacesopenspacesopenspacesopenspace
spacesopenspacesopenspacesopenspacesopenspacesope
openspacesopenspacesopenspacesopenspacesopenspace
spacesopenspacesopenspacesopenspacesopenspacesope
openspacesopenspacesopenspacesopenspacesopenspace
spacesopenspacesopenspacesopenspacesopenspacesope
openspacesopenspacesopenspacesopenspacesopenspace
spacesopenspacesopenspacesopenspacesopenspacesope
openspacesopenspacesopenspacesopenspacesopenspace
spacesopenspacesopenspacesopenspacesopenspacesope
openspacesopenspacesopenspacesopenspacesopenspace
spacesopenspacesopenspacesopenspacesopenspacesope
openspacesopenspacesopenspacesopenspacesopenspace
spacesopenspacesopenspacesopenspacesopenspacesope
openspacesopenspacesopenspacesopenspacesopenspace
spacesopenspacesopenspacesopenspacesopenspacesope
openspacesopenspacesopenspacesopenspacesopenspace
spacesopenspacesopenspacesopenspacesopenspacesope
openspacesopenspacesopenspacesopenspacesopenspace
spacesopenspacesopenspacesopenspacesopenspacesope
openspacesopenspacesopenspacesopenspacesopenspace
spacesopenspacesopenspacesopenspacesopenspacesope
openspacesopenspacesopenspacesopenspacesopenspace
spacesopenspacesopenspacesopenspacesopenspacesope
openspacesopenspacesopenspacesopenspacesopenspace
spacesopenspacesopenspacesopenspacesopenspacesope
openspacesopenspacesopenspacesopenspacesopenspace
spacesopenspacesopenspacesopenspacesopenspacesope
openspacesopenspacesopenspacesopenspacesopenspace
spacesopenspacesopenspacesopenspacesopenspacesope
openspacesopenspacesopenspacesopenspacesopenspace
spacesopenspacesopenspacesopenspacesopenspacesope
openspacesopenspacesopenspacesopenspacesopenspace
spacesopenspacesopenspacesopenspacesopenspacesope
openspacesopenspacesopenspacesopenspacesopenspace
spacesopenspacesopenspacesopenspacesopenspacesope
openspacesopenspacesopenspacesopenspacesopenspace
spacesopenspacesopenspacesopenspacesopenspacesope
openspacesopenspacesopenspacesopenspacesopenspace
spacesopenspacesopenspacesopenspacesopenspacesope
openspacesopenspacesopenspacesopenspacesopenspace
spacesopenspacesopenspacesopenspacesopenspacesope

2020: CPR – OUR HISTORY

Why was the Canadian Pacific Railway built?

Incorporated in 1881, Canadian Pacific Railway was formed
to physically unite Canada and Canadians from coast to coast,
and the building of the railway is considered
to be one of Canada's greatest feats of engineering.

The CPR played a major role in the promotion
of tourism and immigration,
as well as Canada's war efforts
and through the years, the railway grew and diversified
to include steamships,
hotels,
airlines,
mining,
oil and gas exploration,
delivery and telecommunications companies.

1885:
The Métis of
the provisional
government of
Saskatchewan
are attacked by
Canadian soldiers
brought by rail.

2021 Q2:
On strength of safety and
service, CPR reports record
revenues of $2.05 billion.

FRAGMENTS

I

The nest of a Tailorbird is two halves of a broad-leaf stitched—
sewn with spider silk.
The pocket is packed with grass.
Eggs are set in grass.

II

Two Franco-Anglo halves are stitched,
folding in all others.

III

In the *Anglo-Saxon Chronicle* in the entry for the year 449,
the Angles write home to request reinforcements citing
the worthlessness of the Britons and the excellencies of the land.

IV

The CPR advertises:
Get your home in Canada.
Special farms on virgin soil.
Payments in easy installments.

V

Symmetry is a movement operation such that the shape moves
but appears to stay in the same orientation.

PART FOUR

HE WAS ANXIOUS ABOUT THE GLACIERS

1870 Rupert's Land transfer from the Company to the Dominion, the Company retains 5 percent of this territory as well as its most profitable posts.

1871 'Gold may be discovered in paying quantities, any day, on the eastern slope of the Rocky Mountains.'
– W. J. Christie, Chief Factor, In charge of Saskatchewan District, Hudson's Bay Company, Edmonton House

1876 Treaty No. 6 is signed, does not include land now known as Banff National Park.

1877 Treaty No. 7 is signed, includes portions of the land now known as Banff National Park, as with previous treaties, hunting rights are to be upheld.

1880 'The question of the relations of the Dominion of Canada to the Indians of the North-West, is one of great practical importance. The work, of obtaining their good will, by entering into treaties of alliance with them, has now been completed in all the region from Lake Superior to the foot of the Rocky Mountains.'
– Alexander Morris, *The Treaties of Canada with the Indians of Manitoba and the North-West Territories*

1883 CPR track has reached west to what is now known as Lake Louise Station.

1885 October: 'The ground in the vicinity of the springs furnishes unlimited sites for buildings of all descriptions, and should sufficient means be forthcoming, the locality might be made a most attractive one.'
– J. M. Gordon, Agent of Dominion Lands, report to Ottawa

1885 November: 'His Excellency by and with the advice of the Queen's Privy Council for Canada has been pleased to order, and it is hereby ordered, that whereas near the station of Banff on the Canadian Pacific Railway, in the Provisional District of Alberta, North West Territories, there have been discovered several hot mineral springs which promise to be of great sanitary advantage to the public, and in order that proper control of the lands surrounding these springs may be vested in the Crown, the said lands in the territory including said springs and in their immediate neighbourhood, be and they are hereby reserved from sale or settlement or squatting.'
– Order in Council No. 2197

1887 Indigenous peoples forbidden to hunt in the land now known as Banff National Park

1889 A CPR train of tourists is stalled in the park. Citizens of Stoney Nakoda First Nations are requested to perform dances as a means of entertainment. This marks the beginning of what becomes known as the Banff Indian Days festival.

1890 The beginning of removal of First Nations (including Stoney Nakoda) from the land now known as Banff National Park.

1899 Treaty No. 8 is signed, includes remaining land now known as Banff National Park, where resides what remains of the Saskatchewan Glacier.

2010 Stoney Nakoda First Nations 'welcomed' back onto land now known as Banff National Park with the signing of the Memorandum of Understanding.

2012 Citizens of Stoney Nakoda First Nations granted access to lifetime park passes by Parks Canada.

2019 Nakoda Banff Indian Days takes place with the theme: Nakoda Language. Stoney Nakoda First Nations hold ceremony, language and cultural history workshops, storytelling, a round dance, and traditional feast over six days, in the land now known as Banff National Park. Pow wow (open to public visitors): Saturday evening.

YOU COULD THINK OF THIS*

> 'The Geoscience Garden contains types of rock that are important to Canada's landscape and people. They are arranged so as to tell the story of the Earth's crust in Canada ... The rocks are placed so that students of Earth science can learn to make field observations and interpret Earth history.'
>
> – The Geoscience Garden, University of Alberta
> Faculty of Science, Earth and Atmospheric Sciences

As glaciers.
As erratic stones of tremendous stature.
Immovable.
Set, carefully as points amid the prairie.
As stories.
As lessons.

As data.
As a university more immovable than stone,
setting carefully with heavy equipment.
As plaques to tell
what corporation's courtesy brought the mountains
to the campus.

You could think of this as mountains.

You could think of the present shape of the landscape
as a story of how things are and will be again,
as a lesson
as a glacier melting
as a Saskatchewan drainage slowly setting
the silt of mountains.

You could think of this as Edmonton.
As progression.
As the drink of meltwater.
As the flooding
in years of infrequent intensity.
You could think of this as a modulation of the mud.
As where the river flows and bends.

You could think of this as all the water at once.
As moving.
As ice contorting under its own weight and fluid.

---

* 'Many of the informants said water and mountains had not been mentioned at the treaty negotiations.' – John Leonard Taylor, *Two Views on the Meaning of Treaties Six and Seven: An Examination of the Significance of Treaties Six and Seven in the Light of Archival Records and Indian Testimony*

THE GEOLOGY OF COLONIALISM

The Anthropocene
the present catastrophe
made readable in future rock.
This layer in the earth of nuclear waste
mistaken for a strip of what all humans wanted:
a sediment of sharing,
belonging to the world.
To place power and plastic in the earth,
to pry apart the timing points
and layer them in parallel stacks.
To time the earth and make lines of the land,
to offer access to the future's past
as a measurement of warning now –
and not as generations yet to be,
but stacks of pages with gilt edges
on the bookshelves of universities.
To pry apart the timing points –
and label them,
the mark of what is always to be present.
And so it may be said this warming
is no natural process
pulling apart the way things are (with the economy)
from how things got this way (with the land) –
as though this was not precisely the problem being faced –
and so it may be said that this is for each of us
a personal responsibility –
as though we were not on that timeline now –
as though the order of the system were not ordered –
the disorder –
as though diffusion,
whereby a room fills gradually with the scent of a dying thing –

as though diffusion was of an order parallel
with responsibility –
as though dilution was of an order parallel
with the ocean –
as though the process of fossilization and the accumulation of mountains
were of an order parallel with plastic and fission.
The geology of colonialism
is to pry apart the timing points
that separate the atom into polymer lengths –
settle in the earth, and claim it.

OR: TO EXPROPRIATE FROM THE BRITISH MUSEUM'S TRUSTEES

The Anthropocene
is part of everyone's shared heritage
and transcends cultural boundaries.

PARALLELS

I

In ecology: niche –
from Old French, nicher, to nest.

II

In ecology: niche –
occupying a specific habitat and displaying specific
behaviours.

III

In ecology: niche –
a volume of n-dimensions,
each dimension a factor of how the organism lives, thrives.

IV

In ecology: niche –
get access here
this article is only available to subscribers
log in through your institution or purchase.

V

In ecology: niche –
all my relations.

'PROBABLY 80 PERCENT OF THE MOUNTAIN GLACIERS IN ALBERTA AND B.C. WILL DISAPPEAR IN THE NEXT FIFTY YEARS.'

– PROFESSOR DAVID HIK, 2018

'Although we did not know it at the time, we were
standing on probably the only peak in
North America the snows of which, when melted,
find their way into the Pacific, the Arctic, and the
Atlantic oceans; for its glaciers feed
the Columbia,
the Athabasca,
and the Saskatchewan rivers.'

– N. Collie, *Exploration
in the Canadian Rockies*, 1899

'A new world was spread at our feet;
to the westward stretched a vast
ice-field probably never before seen
by human eye,
and surrounded by entirely
unknown,
unnamed,
and unclimbed peaks.'

– H. Stutfield and N. Collie,
*Climbs and Exploration in the Canadian
Rockies*, 1903

'Thus if the quantity of carbonic acid increases in geometric progression, the augmentation of the temperature will increase nearly in arithmetic progression.'

– Svante Arrhenius, *The Greenhouse Gas Law, On the Influence of Carbonic Acid in the Air upon the Temperature of the Ground*, 1896

80 PERCENT OF TH

IS

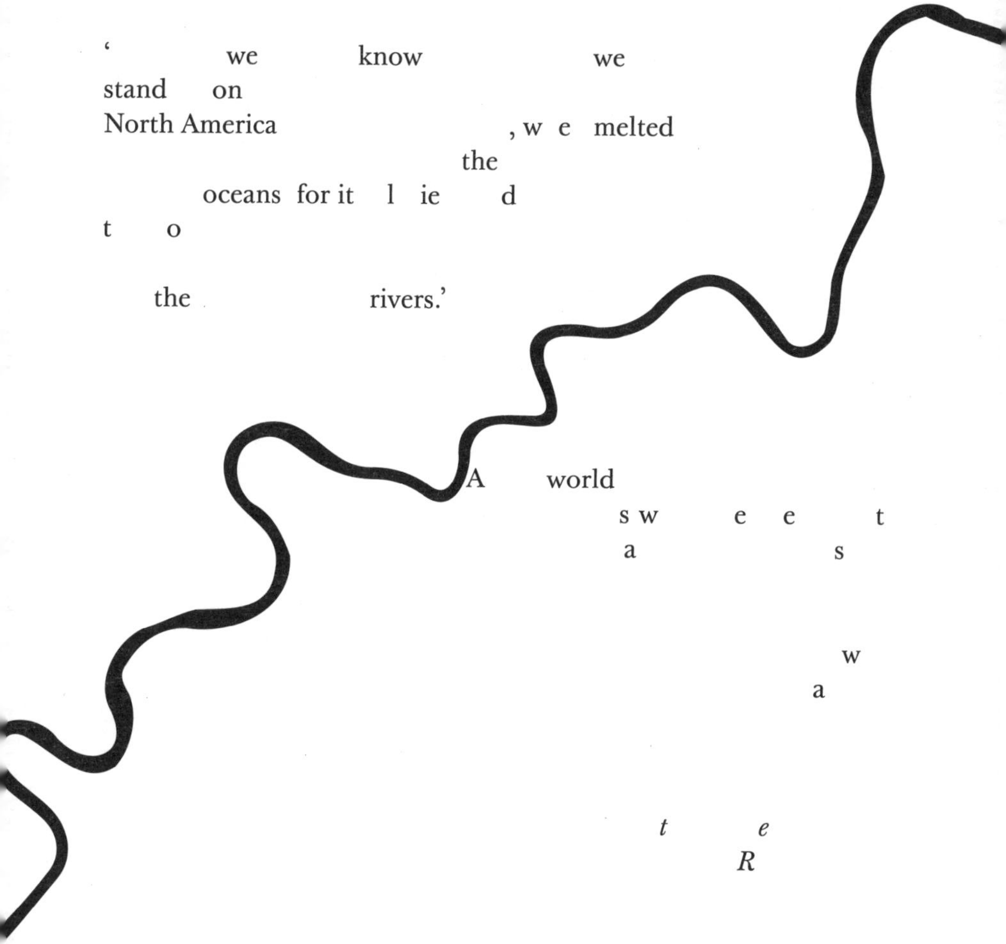

‘ we know we
stand on
North America , w e melted
the
oceans for it l ie d
t o

the rivers.’

A world
s w e e t
a s

w
a

t e
R

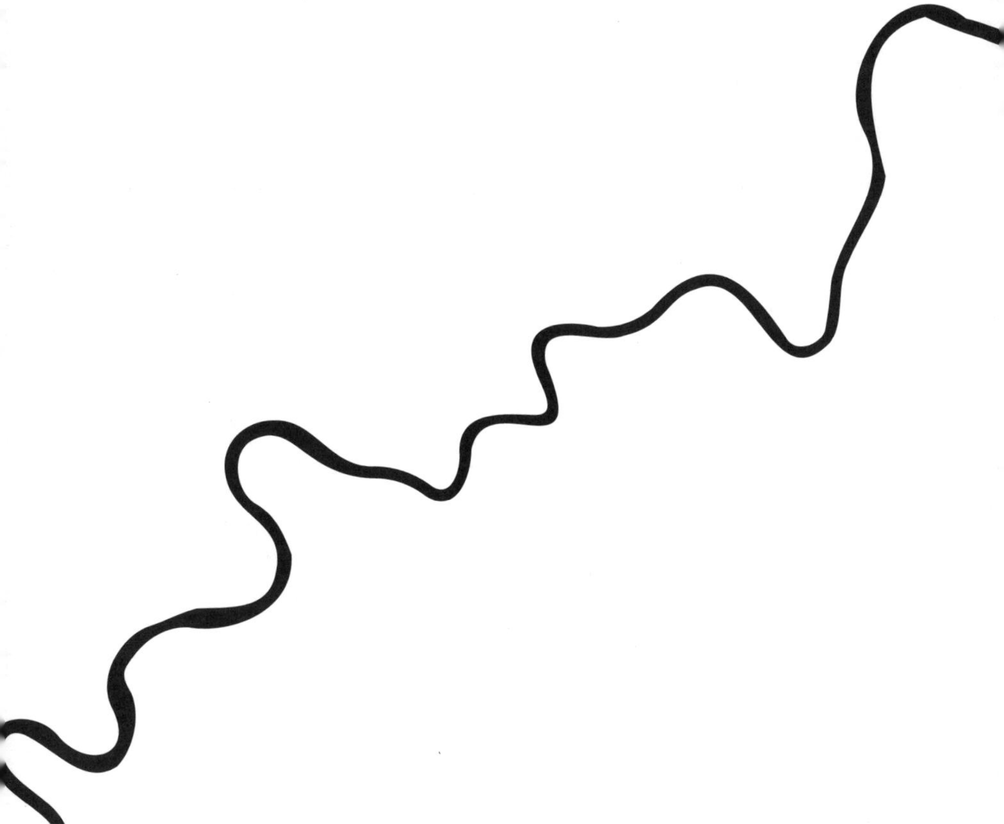

RIVER LOT

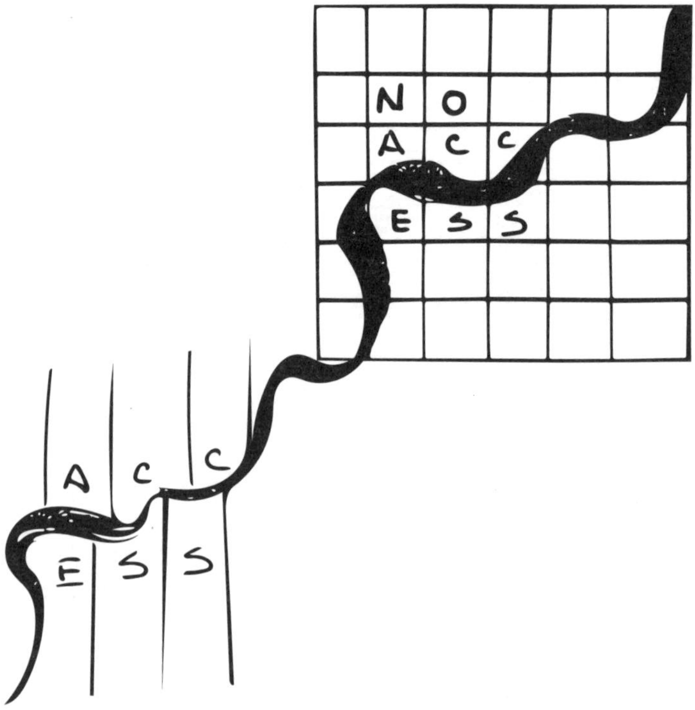

direction of flow

→

AND WHEN IT'S GONE, IT'S GONE

I

To see the buses come to see the ice,
as an empty well might first seem full
for seeing something deeper than oneself.
To see the buses empty, see the train,
to see it fill and full again.
A parking lot of parallel lines.
A window seat. An aisle.
A hollow space to visit something empty
with a feature on the landscape,
first discovered and reported to the royal society
for improving knowledge.

II

To see the families come to see the rock,
as tourists seeing, visiting, and looking
in a farmer's field this time—
and other times and other places, climbing
over this and other storied places,
taking pieces taking even little pieces,
taking any pieces. Stepping,
sliding, grabbing, taking pieces
in the folds of fingerprints, a dust
to palm against the pants to wipe away,
and wiping.
This stone is here as told in stories.
Not as glacier process stories,
stones and icy stories,
but
by a people always here.

THIS IS NOT AN ODE TO THE DAY I FELL OFF MY BIKE AND SKINNED MY KNEE

In the gravel alley behind my cousins' garage, a day the land took a piece of me, and I had learned to ride a bike so late that I did not have the same confidence in momentum that I had in gravity, and when you're a child you hold yourself in an inward way when you cry, in a way you can no longer hold yourself, in the way the land holds you, in an all-limbs-and-all-joints way.

My blood looked so red being strained, in dots, through what was left of skin and dust, and gravel stuck to the knee. It is the land that was stuck to me while I was extruded.

On that day I gave something to the land and I resented giving it up.

This is not an ode to that day or to the day I was bullied and thrown in a lake because I was too small and too fat and too much. A day and many other days I felt so small and not enough.

So although this is an ode to a day in the valley, when I gave to the creek that gave me me, this is not about tobacco, or a lesson from a snake that growth sometimes means you leave a part of yourself behind.

But for that bright day in a lush overwhelming of green in a mosquito summer, where you were not bit as long as you kept moving, with porcupines and a path past depressions in grass where deer had been sleeping. Flowers and driftwood with tiny spiders. Pools with even smaller fish. With water that cut so long into the earth it made a space for all of us.

X

I think about what the phrase 'unspoiled nature' might mean. I question this attitude of parallel existence, of people separated from the landscape in unconverging lines of perpetually maintained distance. How this distance has caused so much pain. I think about how the connections between nations of people and plants and animals have been separated by artificial constructions of thought. How these constructions are perpetuated by structures of living and structures of learning and structures of governance. I think about how the land is living and learning and governance together. How this place beside the creek brings me such joy and knowledge and capacity. That I am Dene and I remember the documentary recording in the University of Alberta archives of my great-grandfather saying:

'The joy of today is not to be spoiled with the fear of tomorrow.
Life is to be lived every moment to the full.'

– James Balsillie

AUTHOR'S ECOLOGY

I have so much to be grateful for, to be here in this place now and doing these things. In honour of the boundless love and faith in me that my parents have relentlessly displayed, I am most grateful to them. I have a lot more to do and a lot more to go, because of you both. The work will be hard, but the going will be joyful and beautiful and I am honoured to do it.

I'm grateful to my grandmother, who showered me with kindness and love and patience and sweetness. I will always remember the lessons she taught me as much as her laughter, her smile, and her great joy.

I am grateful to all my many relations. To my aunties and uncles and my many many cousins here and up north.

It took a lot of community support to write this book.

I am so so grateful for the support of Jordan Abel, mentor, editor, friend. This book couldn't have happened without your guidance and kindness. Also thanks to Keavy Martin, Christine Stewart, Marilyn Dumont, Sarah Krotz, Janet Rogers, Margaret Christakos, Lewis Cardinal, Kristine Smitka, Richard Van Camp, Billy-Ray Belcourt, Liz Howard, Derek Beaulieu, Sally Leys, and many kind librarians, conservators, and archivists for helping me tell my story.

So many friends, new and old, in my community have listened to me work through this project and have all helped to guide and refine it in many ways. I am so grateful to everyone who has shared with me their time, resources, stories, laughter, and kindness. You have inspired, mentored, and supported me in this path of creativity, resistance, and healing. Hunter Cardinal, Jacquelyn Cardinal, Chelsea Fritz, Caitlin Elm, Maria Chen, Al Harding, and many others, especially at school and in the spoken word community.

Nisha, I am so grateful for you and so honoured to share in all this with you.

I love you more than yesterday, but less than tomorrow.

marsi cho.

The author acknowledges grant support from the following organizations: the Canada Council for the Arts, the Edmonton Arts Council, the University of Alberta Office of the Senate Emil Skarin Fund, and the University of Alberta Organization for Arts Students and Interdisciplinary Studies.

Previous versions of these poems were published in 'It Was Treaty / It Was Me,' part of the Vallum Chapbook Series, and *Arc Poetry Magazine*, issue 93.

AUTHOR'S BIOLOGY

Matthew James Weigel is an Edmonton-born and -based Dene and Métis poet and artist.

He holds a Bachelor of Science in Biological Sciences and a Master of Arts in English from the University of Alberta, where he is currently pursuing a PhD in English.

Queer, disabled, former zookeeper and feeder of sharks, sponge aquarist.

Also, the designer for Moon Jelly House press. His words and art have been published by people like *Arc Poetry Magazine*, Book*Hug, *The Polyglot*, and the Mamawi Project. His art can be found in some public places in Edmonton.

He has been a National Magazine Award finalist, shortlisted for the Nelson Ball Prize, and winner of the Cécile E. Mactaggart Award. His collection 'It Was Treaty / It Was Me' won the 2020 Vallum Chapbook Award and the 2021 bpNichol Chapbook Award.

This is his first full-length collection of poetry.

www.matthewjamesweigel.com

Twitter and Instagram: @SpongePoet

Note on the type:
A Baskerville serif typeface was chosen to fit in with the British Museum's display guidelines. The interior sans serif is Social Gothic and Slate Pro. The cover sans serif is Social Gothic.

Printed at the Coach House on bpNichol Lane in Toronto, Ontario, on Zephyr Antique Laid paper, which was manufactured, acid-free, in Saint-Jérôme, Quebec, from second-growth forests. This book was printed with vegetable-based ink on a 1973 Heidelberg KORD offset litho press. Its pages were folded on a Baumfolder, gathered by hand, bound on a Sulby Auto-Minabinda, and trimmed on a Polar single-knife cutter.

Coach House is on the traditional territory of many nations including the Mississaugas of the Credit, the Anishnabeg, the Chippewa, the Haudenosaunee, and the Wendat peoples, and is now home to many diverse First Nations, Inuit, and Métis peoples. We acknowledge that Toronto is covered by Treaty 13 with the Mississaugas of the Credit. We are grateful to live and work on this land.

Edited by Jordan Abel
Cover design by Crystal Sikma, cover art by Matthew James Weigel
Interior design by Matthew James Weigel
Author photo by HueandSun Photography

Coach House Books
80 bpNichol Lane
Toronto ON M5S 3J4
Canada

416 979 2217
800 367 6360

mail@chbooks.com
www.chbooks.com